EUROPE
FOR THE HURRIED TOURIST

Alexandre Digmeloff

outskirts press

Denver, Colorado

The opinions expressed in this manuscript are solely the opinions of the author and do not represent the opinions or thoughts of the publisher. The author has represented and warranted full ownership and/or legal right to publish all the materials in this book.

Europe Digest For The Hurried Tourist
All Rights Reserved.
Copyright © 2012 Alexandre Digmeloff
v4.0

Cover Photo © 2012 JupiterImages Corporation.
All rights reserved - used with permission.

This book may not be reproduced, transmitted, or stored in whole or in part by any means, including graphic, electronic, or mechanical without the express written consent of the publisher except in the case of brief quotations embodied in critical articles and reviews.

Outskirts Press, Inc.
http://www.outskirtspress.com

ISBN: 978-1-4327-7533-9

Library of Congress Control Number: 2011929538

Outskirts Press and the "OP" logo are trademarks belonging to Outskirts Press, Inc.

PRINTED IN THE UNITED STATES OF AMERICA

Contents

INTRODUCTION 1
EUROPE 11
THE EUROPEAN UNION 13

AUSTRIA 17
VIENNA 25
SALZBURG 34
INNSBRUCK 41

FRANCE 47
THE FRENCH 48
PARIS 61
REIMS AND THE CATHEDRAL 99
PROVENCE - CÔTE D'AZUR 101
ARLES 103
NIMES 105
AVIGNON 108
MARSEILLE 109
CANNES, NICE, AND THE FRENCH RIVIERA 116

GERMANY 135
FRANKFURT- AM- MAIN 149
HEIDELBERG 151
MUNICH 157
NEUSCHWANSTEIN AND LOUIS II 167
BERCHSTESGADEN 168

ROTHENBURG OB DER TAUBER 171

GREAT BRITAIN 179
LONDON 188
THE THAMES RIVER.. 209
CANTERBURY AND DOVER 211

ITALY 215
THE ITALIANS 219
ROME 232
TUSCANY AND FLORENCE 249
PISA 259
SIENA.. 262
UMBRIA.. 265
BOLOGNA.. 269
PADUA 273
VENICE 275

SWITZERLAND 295
LUCERNE 305
ON THE ROAD FROM LUCERNE TO GOTTHARD 311

ADDITIONAL WEB RESOURCES 315
BIBLIOGRAPHY 317

INTRODUCTION

WHEN VISITING EUROPE with an organized tour, the tour manager and the local guides provide the tourist with the necessary information as the journey proceeds. However, if some circuits allow periods of rest and leisure for personal activities, some others – generally student or budget tours – are designed to go at a frantic pace, resulting from an unrealistic program sold to the client, listing a maximum possible number of places "visited", even if it means ridiculously little time for each visit. Free time is reduced to a minimum, and when left on his own, the hurried tourist will find difficult to choose the best amongst the variety of activities, shops, or restaurants.

The individual traveler is somewhat more at ease, since his timetable may be more flexible, but he is certainly eager on making the proper choices, especially when he comes to Europe for the first time.

Of course, it is greatly recommended, before departure, to gather some knowledge of the countries, towns, and people one will see and meet.

However, there are hundreds of travel books, sometimes costly, and thousands of publications on the Net. How not to be submerged with this more or less reliable mass of information?

This pocket-sized road book focuses on the six most visited countries: Austria, France, Germany, Great Britain, Italy, and Switzerland.

It does not take in account the organization of the trip, or the booking of hotels, transfers, etc. The Travel Agent or the Tour Operator provides this service.

It does not cover every place extensively, and has reduced the necessary knowledge to the strict minimum.

Whether you are traveling as an individual, or as a group, this book will help you to meet local people, gain their respect, and avoid misunderstanding or mistreatment. It intends to give the visitor a secure feeling by teaching him or her how to avoid typical tourist blunders.

It also gives ideas and hints for a basic visiting program, including shopping and eating, for those who want to see and experience la crème de la crème in minimum time and, when back home, talk brilliantly about their trip.

ADVICE BEFORE VISITING EUROPE

CURRENCY EXCHANGE

THERE MIGHT BE a substantive difference between the official and the actual local currency exchange, as the inter-bank rate does not take into account the commission of local banks and exchange offices. Great Britain and Switzerland have kept their national currency, the Sterling Pound (£) and the Swiss Franc, respectively, but all other countries in this book have adopted the Euro.

Before you leave, consult a web site such as:
www.Oanda.com/currency/converter.

The best possible rate can be obtained from one's own bank at home when purchasing foreign currency in cash or travelers' checks. However, this requires you to carry the money with you, which is not very safe. All over the trip, the best way is to use a credit card, as your bank will then debit your account at a fair rate. Visa cards are accepted in all countries, and cash money distributors are found everywhere. American Express is less frequently accepted, and cash distributors are rare.

When in Europe, travelers will find scores of banks, exchange offices, or booths, mainly situated in the city shopping center. The difference between one exchange office and another can be significant, and official banks do not always offer the best rate. If time allows, visit three of four banks or exchange booths (they are usually not far from each other – for instance Piccadilly in London, rue Scribe, near the Opera and in front of the Intercontinental Grand Hotel in Paris, city-center in Lucerne) to find the one offering a rate of exchange as close as possible to the interbank rate.

The Airport exchange booths sometimes offer fair rates, but not always.

Never, under any circumstances, exchange money on the street. The time when one could get more than the value of the official rate is history. Currencies are now stable; accepting an offer from a street vendor means a probability to being cheated.

TAX REFUND

Travelers whose habitual residence is outside of the European Union are entitled to the V.A.T. refund on the purchases that they make. The V.A.T. is different from one country to another: the lowest tax is 8 % in Switzerland, the highest is 25 % in Scandinavian countries. Other countries treated in this book have the following rates:

Austria: 20 %
France: 19.6 %
Germany: 19 %
Great Britain: 20 %
Italy: 20 %

According to customs regulations varying slightly from one country to the other, the amount of goods purchased in a single shop on the same day must be around 170 €. Not all products are eligible and not all retailers offer tax-free shopping. Retailers who practice the tax refund system usually provide all of the necessary information and forms needed.

PICKPOCKETS

They exist since antiquity and will probably exist until the end of the universe.

Many texts from ancient Rome mention their existence, and medieval chronicles report the fruitful activity of purse-snatchers and other crooks.

No country is immune to pickpockets, although Northern Europe and Switzerland seem to suffer less damage than the Southern states. London, Barcelona, Paris and the Côte d'Azur, Italy's main cities, and Vienna are particularly plagued, especially since opening borders with

Eastern European states. The situation is so dire that France, Italy, and Germany are taking measures to expel gypsies. In the second half of 2010, France expelled several thousands of gypsies – which is vehemently criticized by well-thinkers. They will probably return in a few months…

One of the gypsy methods is to surround the visitor with a group of five to eight young boys or girls and distract him whilst his pockets are visited. The youngsters, aged 8 to 14 years, have been trained since childhood to that sort of operation, and are incredibly swift.

Durant and Cheryl Imboden, give the following remarks on their web site veniceforvisitors.com:

"Most thefts occur because people make careless (and easily avoided) mistakes such as:

- Carrying wallets in hip-pockets, where they're easy for a pickpocket to reach.
- Wearing purses over and behind the shoulder.
- Storing valuables in hip-pouches or "fanny packs."
- Stuffing mobile phones, passports, and other valuables in backpacks.
- Carrying heavy camera bags (or, worse yet, obvious camera backpacks) that might as well be labeled "Steal me."
- Resting handbags on top of luggage while concentrating on a map or guidebook.
- Hanging purses from chair backs in cafés and restaurants.
- Wearing "neck wallets" outside clothing, in full

view of thieves, instead of hidden inside a shirt or blouse."

Pickpockets are not dangerous, but being careful about your belongings, especially when mingled with a crowd in a public place, will certainly avoid the inconvenience of losing your wallet, purse, passport, and other valuables, and ruin the pleasure of your trip.

EUROPE

EUROPE

THE NAME EUROPE comes from Greek mythology.

As told by Homer, Europa was the beautiful daughter of Agenor, King of Phoenicia (the old name of Lebanon). One day, while she was tending her father's flock near Tyr, a splendid milk-white bull appeared before her. Europa decked his horns with flowers and, as she stroked it, mounted on its broad back. The bull stood up, plunged with Europa into the sea, and swam to the island of Crete. The bull, who was in fact Zeus (Jupiter for the Romans) in disguise, vanished and the God appeared to Europa in full glory. From their union was born Minos, who became king of Crete. He created the Minoan civilization, which was named after him and lasted from around 3,000 to 1,100 B.C.

It was the origin of the Greek civilization. As Zeus brought Europa to them, the Greeks decided to give her name to their continent. Europe covers a surface of 10 million km2 (380,000 sq mi) and stretches 2,480 miles north to south and 3,410 miles east to west. More than 40 countries compose the continent. In the final decade of the 20th

EUROPE DIGEST FOR THE HURRIED TOURIST

century, Europe was home to 700 million inhabitants.

The frontiers between states, which do not always coincide with national boundaries, show more and more instability, as national minorities demand their autonomy or independence. The latest examples of such conflicts are the fights of Kurds and Kosovars against a state to which they do not belong either by language or by religion. Other examples include the demands of the minorities once under the Soviet regime and now liberated in post-communist Eastern Europe as well as the "velvet-divorce" obtained by the Slovak nationalist movement, separating them from the Czech Republic in 1992-93. This ethnic problem was created mainly by the Treaty of Versailles, imposed by the winning states and remodeling Europe without the slightest concern for ethnic settlements or partitions, which led, amongst others, to brutal annexations by the Bolsheviks in Eastern Europe and central Asia. An example of this non-respect of ethnical rights is the deportation to Siberia of 80% of the Chechen population when they rose against their annexation by the U.S.S.R.

In the last 40 years, the economically rich Western European countries have also attracted a large number of immigrants, creating new minorities and social tensions. Due to the Schengen Agreement signed in 1985, all customs and police controls have been suppressed on the boarders for European Union members, except Norway, Iceland, United Kingdom and Ireland. Switzerland, although not a member of the European Union, joined the block's passport-free travel zone in 2008.

Consequently, the flow of migrant workers is very difficult to stem. Illegal immigration is flourishing on the coasts of Spain and Italy. Albanians, North, West, and Central Africans, swarm into France, Belgium, and Germany. People from Afghanistan and other Asian sub-continental migrants try desperately to cross over to England.

THE EUROPEAN UNION

The European Community was founded in 1957 as a Common Market, later named the European Union. The borders of member countries were eliminated in 1993; the creation of a large single market stimulated trade, fuelled by a common currency, the Euro, launched in 2001. Launched in February 1995 with 17 members, the EU has been joined in 2004 by 10 new members, which makes it even more difficult to administer. Members of the E.U. are Austria, Belgium, Bulgaria, Cyprus, Czech Republic, Denmark, Estonia, Finland, France, Germany, Great Britain, Greece, Hungary, Ireland, Italy, Latvia, Lithuania, Luxembourg, Malta, Netherlands, Poland, Portugal, Romania, Slovakia, Slovenia, Spain, and Sweden. Three countries are candidates to join: Croatia, Macedonia, and Turkey.

AUSTRIA

AUSTRIA

AUSTRIA IS A federal state consisting of nine autonomous provinces based on the Swiss model, which was adopted in 1920. Austria covers an area of 32,500 sq. miles. Its population is 7.5 million inhabitants, 1.2 million of which live in Vienna.

Main cities are Vienna, the capital; Graz, the capital of the Kärnten province; Salzburg, the birthplace of Wolfgang Amadeus Mozart; and Innsbrück, the capital of Austrian Tyrol.

The Austrian Federal Government (Bundesregierung) is the Austrian cabinet. It consists of the Chancellor, Vice Chancellor, as well as the federal ministers. The President and the government form the federal executive. The Chancellor presides over government meetings. Federal ministers are responsible for a ministry on their own title, not that of the total government.

Austria presents a great variety of sceneries: from the snow-capped Tyrolean Alps and scores of winter-sport resorts, to its magnificent lakes, and down to the Danube

EUROPE DIGEST FOR THE HURRIED TOURIST

Valley, with medieval castles and vineyards. For centuries, Austria's command of vital east-west and north-south trade routes gave it both commercial and strategic importance. The Danube River links Western and Eastern Europe; north-south Alpine passes connect the country with the Mediterranean and the Balkans.

Austria is basically Germanic in language and ethnic affiliation, although its eastern part has gradually come under the influence of Central-European ethnic groups. The minorities include about 40,000 Croats, principally in Burgenland, about 70,000 Slovenes, concentrated in southern Carinthia, and small groups of Hungarians (about 11,000 and Czechs (about 5,000). All citizens are covered by national health insurance. In the late 19th and early 20th centuries, Vienna was Europe's perhaps greatest medical center, known particularly for the development of modern psychiatry laid by Sigmund Freud.

Austria is the country of winter sports, and the national sport is skiing.

Facilities include 75 winter sports resorts – 13,700 miles of ski slopes – 147 cable cars – 2,700 ski tows – 512 chair lifts – 528 ski schools with 8,300 ski instructors.

About 25 million foreign visitors come to Austria every year, 1 million of which are from the United States.

HISTORY

Austria descends from a mighty empire. In the 16th century, the Habsburg dynasty governed Germany, Southern

AUSTRIA

Italy, Slovenia, Croatia, Bohemia and Slovaquia, Hungary, The Netherlands, Spain, and Portugal, and their respective colonies in South America. In ancient times, much of the territories, later known collectively as "Austria," (Eastern Land = Österreich), were called Rhaetia, Noricum, and Pannonia. They were organized as Roman provinces in the 1st century AD. For the next 10 centuries, the area served the more civilized peoples of Europe – initially Roman, later Frankish and German – as a defensive outpost against barbarian invasions from the east (the Eastern March).

Roman control collapsed in the 4th century under wave after wave of Germanic and Hunnish invaders. In the 6th century, these tribes were joined by Slavs and Avars, over whom the Franks established, under CHARLEMAGNE, a brief ascendancy in the 8th century.

Charlemagne became the first Holy Roman Emperor invested by the Pope as the protector of Christian Faith in Europe. When the last of the Carolingians disappeared without an heir, the rulers of the Four Nations (Swabia, Franconia, Bavaria and Saxony) assembled to elect the King of Germany. They were to be known as Grand Electors. The crown was given to a Frank, and then passed to Saxons, then back again to Franks. Nomads from the east, among them Magyars (Hungarians), continued to overrun the Danubian area.

Otto I, later Holy Roman emperor, defeated them in the mid-10th century and reorganized the eastern border region and Austria as a dependency of the dukes of Bavaria. Austria, which began as the region between

EUROPE DIGEST FOR THE HURRIED TOURIST

Salzburg and Vienna, was ruled for two and a half centuries by the Dynasty of the Babenberg. They extended the country east to the Hungarian border and south over Styria and Carinthia (Steirmark and Kärnten). When the last of the Babenberg, Frederick the Warrior, was killed fighting against the Magyars, the duchy throne was left vacant and aroused the envy of the Kings of Bohemia and Hungary. Ottokar II, King of Bohemia finally prevailed and became Duke of Austria and Styria in 1250. Fifteen years later, Rudolf VON HABSBURG, who had been elected King of Germany by the German Princes, rose against Ottokar, whom he defeated. He was the founder of the Habsburg dynasty and ruled over Austria and two thirds of Europe until 1914. The Habsburgs turned Austria into one of the most dynamic states of Europe. The most preeminent figures of that dynasty were:

- Maximilian I, was elected Holy Roman Emperor and married Mary of Burgundy, sole heiress of the Duchy of Burgundy, bringing this powerful and rich territory into the Habsburg purse; he married his eldest son, Phillip the Handsome, to the Infant of Spain. Their son, Charles, became one of the most powerful kings of all times.

- Charles V was crowned King of Germany and Roman Holy Emperor as the successor of Maximilian in 1519, simply by inheriting from his various ascendants: he so acquired Spain and Portugal and their possessions in South America,

AUSTRIA

Burgundy, the Netherlands and Belgium, the kingdoms of Naples, Sicily and Sardinia, Austria, some smaller territories in southern Germany, as well as hereditary claims to the crowns of Bohemia and Hungary, which were to be gained later by his younger brother, Ferdinand. It was really an Empire on which "the sun was never setting down".

- Maria Theresia, daughter of Charles VI Habsburg, became extremely popular for her financial and administrative reforms and her influence on art and architecture. She had sixteen children, including Marie-Antoinette, who later married the King of France Louis XIV and was assassinated by the French revolutionaries.

The Austro-Hungarian Empire collapsed definitively in 1914 when Archduke Franz Ferdinand, heir to the throne, was murdered by Serb nationalists in Sarajevo. This ignited the First World War (the Austrian generals were absolutely sure they would liquidate Serbia in 8 days ...), and the defeat of German-Austrian armies after four years of horrible fighting.

Annexed by Germany in 1938 (the Anschluss) and occupied by the Allies after World War II, Austria has been a neutral state since 1955. It became a founding member of the European Free Trade Association in 1959 and formally applied to join the European Community in 1990.

Austrians are fierce traditionalists. They are very proud of their culture and education and try to keep their traditions alive. Men often wear loden olive green or gray jackets, sometimes leather pants, and hats with pheasant feathers, while women wear the traditional dirndl, a dress made of cloth printed with a multitude of small flowers.

AUSTRIAN ART AND CULTURE

Austria gave the world and European culture great music composers, such as Joseph Haydn, Franz Schubert, Anton Bruckner, Gustav Mahler, and the two Johan Strauss (the Elder and the Younger), renowned for their world famous waltzes (The Beautiful Blue Danube), and Operettas, such as the Gipsy Baron.

From 1815 to 1850, musical entertainment was prevalent, and waltz was danced everywhere, from the Emperor's Court to the little taverns in the vineyards. Beethoven and Brahms also composed some of their best works in Vienna.

Of course, the best-known Austrian musician is Wolfgang Amadeus Mozart. Born in Salzburg in 1756, Mozart was a naturally gifted child prodigy. At the age of 14, he was appointed concertmaster of the archbishop's orchestra in Salzburg. Although most famous for Don Giovanni and Figaro's wedding, he composed about 1,000 pieces, only 70 of which were published before he died. The Viennese public greeted his greatest works with incomprehension, and he died poor at the age of 35. He was buried with the poor, and the place of his burial has never been found.

Arnold Schönberg founded the New Viennese School,

AUSTRIA

which proclaimed a musical revolution. Another great Austrian musician, Herbert von Karajan, was a conductor of the greatest symphonic orchestras.

Other fields where Austria has enriched the world are literature and science. Franz Kafka (1883-1924) was born in Prag, which was then part of the Austrian Empire. Other famous names include Rainer Maria Rilke, Stefan Zweig, Arthur Schnitzler, Robert von Musil, and Hugo von Hofmannsthal. Sigmund Freud was born in Moravia (now part of the Czech Republic) in 1856. Austrians have also initiated new developments in furniture and architectural styles.

Biedermeyer furniture is world-renowned and reaches fabulous prices in auction sales.

Jugendstil originated in Munich at the end of 19th century and found its achievement in Austria with the painter Gustav Klimt and the architect Otto Wagner. Oskar Kokoshka and Egon Schiele, leaders of what was later known as Viennese Expressionism, founded modern painting.

Johann Strauss (1825 -1899)

June 3, 2009 marked the 110th anniversary of the death of Johann Strauss, the Emperor of the Waltz. Strauss was born on October 25, 1826 in the Vienna suburbs. His father, also named Johann, was a well-known musician and composer with his own orchestra. He did not want his son to become a musician and enrolled him at the Polytechnikum to study finance and banking. If the father had prevailed,

EUROPE DIGEST FOR THE HURRIED TOURIST

Johann Strauss would have never had anything to do with music. But he had no fancy for his studies and was expelled after two years. Strauss showed his musical talent very early and composed his first waltz at the age of six. His mother encouraged him, and he took violin lessons in secret. At 19, he debuted his own orchestra at a wine restaurant in Hietzing in the suburb of Vienna, and was immediately granted with big success. From that moment, there were two Johann Strauss orchestras in Vienna, and the son went even in competition with his father. When his father died in 1849, he took over his orchestra, and merged it with his own. During the golden days that followed, he wrote numerous famous waltzes, including the "On the Wonderful Blue Danube" waltz. Pushed by his fellow composer Offenbach, he also composed operettas such as "Fledermaus" (the bat) in 1874, "One night in Venice" 1833, and "The Gipsy Baron" 1855. He toured Europe extensively, playing before Queen Victoria, and went for a tour of America in 1872. Upon his return to Vienna, he composed "The Centennial Waltz," which he dedicated to the citizens of America on the 100th anniversary of the Declaration of Independence. Only 12 days before his death, he conducted his orchestra for the first time at the Vienna State Opera.

AUSTRIA

VIENNA

WHAT TO SEE AND DO

Much information can be found on the official Vienna site: wien.info/en

Kärtner Strasse

The center of Vienna, this fashionable shopping pedestrian street runs from the Opera House to the Saint Stevens Cathedral and offers, all around the area, numerous shops, including the new big Swarowski Center, coffeehouses, and restaurants.

Prater

At this lively entertainment park, take a ride on the Riesenrad, a giant wheel constructed in 1867 and made famous worldwide by Orson Welles's film "The Third Man." It provides a romantic experience, and a breathtaking view of the city.

For more information, visit: riesenrad.com

The Ring Boulevard

Take a ride on Tram n° 1 or 2 before exploring the inner city. The route follows the large boulevard built on the former Vienna fortifications, dismantled in the 19th century, surrounding the city center and lined with monumental buildings. An alternative is to ride on a vintage tram: Saturdays, Sundays and Holidays at 11:30 and 13:30 from Karlsplatz. Tickets at the Wiener Linien (Vienna Lines) counter in the Karlsplatz underground station.

Transport is cheaper with a « Wien Karte »: for 18.50 €, you get 72 hours unlimited free transport on buses, trams and the underground + discount coupons in museums, cafés, restaurants, the "Heurige Taverns"(see hereafter), or for shopping. It is available in hotels, at the tourist information centers, and at sales and information points of the Vienna Lines (e.g. Stephansplatz, Karlsplatz, Westbahnhof, Landstraße/Wien Mitte)

Spanische Reitschule

The Spanish Riding School is a part of Austria's cultural heritage, and the oldest riding academy in the world. The School is named "Spanish" after the horses, which originated from the Iberian Peninsula during the 16th century. Today's Lipizzaner stallions are the descendants of this Spanish breed, a cross between Spanish, Arabian and Berber horses, and they delight horse lovers from all over the world with their performances.

Tickets to this famous Spanish riding school must be bought in advance at Hofburg or through a theater ticket agency.

Rent a Bike

Guided tours are available by calling 1-319-12-58.

AUSTRIA

Flea Market
Saturdays along the Danube Canal (Schwedenplatz-Marienbrücke).

Sit in an Old Coffee House, and sip Viennese coffee with pastries, croissants or a slice of Sacher Torte (see further below): the choice of coffees is remarquable (some 30 preparations are available). For instance:

- Kleiner / grosser Schwarzer: small / large cup of black coffee,
- Verlängter Schwarzer /Brauner: diluted with water,
- Melange: milky coffee Kapuziner: cappuccino (with whipped cream),
- Kaffee verkehrt: coffee with more milk than coffee ,
- Mazagran: iced coffee with rhum ,
- Türkischer Kaffee: classical Turkish coffee,
- Flaker: black coffee in a glass with a tot of rhum,

And many more variations…

The Viennese coffeehouse
On July 14, 1683, a Turkish army 300,000 invaded Central Europe and lay siege to Vienna for the second time. The city resisted all attacks for two months until other European kingdoms – including the Poles, Saxons, Bavarians, Swabians, and Franconians – arrived to the rescue on September 10. Caught between two forces, the Turks retreated in panic two days later. G. Kolschitzky, a Turkish interpreter, was rewarded for his heroism with 500

sacks of coffee found in the army supplies abandoned by the Turks. He was also granted the exclusive license to open Vienna's first coffeehouse. He altered the method of preparing Turkish coffee by adapting it to the taste of the Viennese: milk was added, and the *Wiener melange* was born. In memory of the victory over the Turks, Kolschitzky served coffee with small pastries in the shape of the Turkish crescent, which later became known as croissants. In 1700, Emperor Leopold I granted license to sell coffee to four other restaurant owners. By the mid-18th century, coffeehouses had become extremely popular and served as the meeting points for discussions of politics, economy, art, and culture. At the Viennese exhibition in 1873, the coffeehouse became famous to visitors from all over the world. Throughout Europe, many coffeehouses took the Viennese style as a model.

Café Central, founded by Kolschitzky, is the oldest coffeehouse in Vienna, a beautiful place full of character and history (Herrengasse 14).

WHERE AND WHAT TO EAT

Local and international food can be found everywhere. However, a nice experience is to go to a Keller, (usually a vaulted underground cellar), to enjoy the atmosphere, often with Austrian or Gipsy music, and eat Viennese food.

Viennese Cuisine is the only cuisine in the world to be named after a city.

Vienna has been for centuries a melting point of influ-

AUSTRIA

ences from Italy, France, and various regions of the former Austro-Hungarian Empire. As multitudes of immigrants made their way into Vienna, Viennese Chefs have adopted many foreign receipts, adding their own personal touch.

Typical Viennese specialties include:

Wiener Schnitzel:
Specialty originating from the Italian "*costoletta milanese*", it consists of a thin fillet of veal fried in breadcrumbs, usually served with warm or cold potato salad.

Rostbraten, sauerkraut und knoedel (pork roast, sauerkraut, and dumpling).

Gulasch
Hungarian soup or a stew spiced with paprika and garnished with tomatoes

Palatschinken
Hungarian thinly rolled pancakes served with different fillings and toppings, such as apple, cherries, or fresh cream cheese.

Strudel
Puff pastry turnover filled with apples, cherries, or white cheese.

Sacher Torte: chocolate cake covered with chocolate

icing and a layer of apricot jam. Invented by Franz Sacher in 1832 when he was an apprentice in Prince Metternich's kitchen, this dessert made him famous and rich, and enabled his second son, Eduard, to open the Hotel Sacher in 1876. This hotel, facing the Vienna Opera, is of course the best place to enjoy a slice of Sacher Torte.

KELLERS

Augustinerkeller

Augustinerstrasse 1 (inner city, just behind the Opera house). Tel: 01 5331026

Built in the basement of the historic fortifications surrounding the old city, this is one of the last monastic wine cellars in central Vienna, with a vaulted brick ceiling, wooden "cow-stall" booths, street lanterns, Austrian bric-a-brac, and roaming musicians in the evening, playing *schrammel* (traditional Viennese music). Austro-Hungarian or Bavarian food is excellent, as well as local wines, and prices are very affordable

Esterhazykeller

(Haarhof - near Naglergasse, at the west end of Graben, the large street that intersects with Kärtner Strasse.) Tel: 015333482

This is another 17th century old *gemütlich* (cozy) vaulted cellar, located in the basement of the Esterhazy palace. Traditional Viennese food is at its best and prices very reasonable.

AUSTRIA

Gulasch Museum
Schulerstrasse 20 Tel: 01512 1017

As the name indicates, this restaurant focuses on the national Hungarian dish and celebrates at least 15 varieties of it, all widely using the national spice, paprika. You can order versions of goulash made with roast beef, veal, pork, or even fried chicken livers. There is even a version for vegetarians. Prices average € 10.

Heurigen

Another typical experience is to try one of the famous taverns, originally wine cellars, called *Heurigen* (heuer means "today's, new"), which serve wines from their own production of the year. They are located in the villages on the forested hills west of the city. The best choices are the villages Grinzing, Heiligenstadt and Nussdorf, These three old villages, now incorporated into the Vienna urban area, are easily reachable by tram or bus. The typical old-time look has been preserved, and many wine taverns line the streets, offering excellent fare and a choice of the famous white wines, such as Grüner Veltliner, Müller-Thurgau, and Gumpoldskirchen. There is often music, and on sunny days, one can seat outside in the garden.

Johan Strauss son started his career in Hietzing, another wine village.

EUROPE DIGEST FOR THE HURRIED TOURIST

Mayer am Pfarrplatz
Pfarrplatz 2, Nussdorf, Wien 1119
Tel. 01 370 1287
www.pfarrplatz.at

Cobblestone courtyards and historical buildings – one of which housed Ludwig van Beethoven in 1817. Mayer am Pfarrplatz is one of the oldest and most attractive Heurige. The wine also has a reputation for being one of the city's best.

WHAT TO BUY

Loden is a woven fabric of Tyrolean origin, made of a thick, water resistant woolen material with a short pile. First produced by peasants from Austria, it is derived from the coarse, oily wool of mountain sheep and has an olive-green color. Loden coats and jackets are light to wear, warm and comfortable.

Dirndl is a type of traditional dress worn in southern Germany, Liechtenstein, and Austria, based on the historical costumes of Alpine peasants. The dirndl originated as a simplified form of folk costume. It was once the uniform of Austrian servants in the 19th century (*dirndlgewand* means "maid's dress"). The Austrian upper classes adopted the dirndl as high fashion in the 1870s. Today, dirndls vary from simple styles to exquisitely crafted, very expensive models. Specialized loden and dirndl shops are located at Kärtner Str.10 – Kärtner Str.29/31 – Michaelerplatz 6 – Schottengasse 3a.

AUSTRIA

Swarowski crystals

There is no need to introduce the world's most famous manufacturer of crystal jewelry (formerly called "strass"). From a small crystal-cutting company founded in 1895, Daniel Swarovski built an empire in the design and production of crystal jewelry and accessories. Today, the company is managed by fourth and fifth generation family members. The main Swarowski shop in Vienna is located on Kärtnerstrasse 8.

Piatnik playing cards

Piatnik is known around the world for excellent playing cards. For over 185 years, the card-painting business has become an industrial enterprise and is still run by Ferdinand Piatnick's descendants.

SALZBURG

Salzburg, the capital city of the eponymous Austrian federal state, is situated near the foothills of the Alps and the border of Germany, about 270 km (170 mi) west of Vienna. The city's population is 140,000. Salzburg's name is derived from the area's rich salt deposits. Industrial products include musical instruments, beer, hardware, and textiles. Salzburg welcomes large numbers of tourists drawn not only by the scenery of the surrounding Salzach Valley but also by the city's architectural and cultural assets. The town is dominated by the large and well-preserved fortress of Hohensalzburg (1077m), which is easily reachable by funicular railway. Salzburg's present architectural splendor is largely the result of extensive building by the prince archbishops and wealthy burghers of the 16th to 18th centuries. Because these buildings show an Italian influence, Salzburg has been called the "German Rome."

Above all, the city is known for its musical heritage. Wolfgang Amadeus Mozart was born and composed in Salzburg. A world famous musical festival takes place in Salzburg in August. Works of Mozart are played along with those of other composers, including modern ones. The festival was directed by the conductor Herbert von Karajan for many years. The "rococo" castle Leopoldskron (1736) is the current location of the Salzburg Seminar in American Studies.

AUSTRIA

Baroque and rococo styles

"Baroque" is the name given to the art and architecture of Europe and its Latin American colonies in the 17th and the first half of the 18th centuries.

The word may be derived from *"baroco,"* a scholastic term coined as a mnemonic aid for a tortuous argument in logic. As used by late 18th-century art critics, it signified absurd, willful, or grotesque – in other words, a wanton defiance of the classical rules.

Baroque artists and architects created some, although not many, entirely new forms, of which perhaps the most important was the double curve – inward at the sides, outward in the middle – used for facades, doorways, and furniture. Other primary architectural features include twisted columns and fantastical pediments. The building facades show a contrast of dark and light colors, mainly grey, beige, light brown.

The sculptural style is characterized by fluttering draperies, realistic surfaces, and the use of bronze, white, and colored marble. In painting, the main features are illusionistic ceilings and a new kind of realism enhanced by the use of light and shade.

The development of the baroque style began in Italy around 1600. The first to turn this into a definite aesthetic style, however, was the Flemish painter Rubens, who, after studying in Italy from 1600 to 1608, created a style of marvelous color, vitality, and realism. He used the style in paintings for the Roman Catholic Church and for the court in his native country; he also practiced it while visiting the courts of Paris, Madrid, and London.

In France, full acceptance of the baroque was hindered by the prevailing cult of reason, which favored classical restraint, but the resulting classical-baroque style produced the greatest of all royal palaces, Versailles (1669-1703). In Protestant England, a temperate form of baroque was applied in the design of large country houses and, most notably, St. Paul's Cathedral in London.

Rococo style

The term "*rococo*" refers to a style of decoration in Europe, particularly France, during the 18th century. It applies both to interior decoration and to ornaments. By extension, it may also be applied to some sculptures, paintings, furniture, and architectural details, although hardly to architecture as such.

"Rococo" derives from the French word "rocaille," meaning the bits of rocky decoration sometimes found in 16th-century architectural schemes. It was first used in its modern sense around 1800, at about the same time as baroque, and was also initially a pejorative term.

In a typical rococo decorative scheme, series of tall wooden panels (including the doors), decorated with brilliantly inventive carved and gilded motifs in low relief, are arranged around the room. After 1720, the panels were usually painted ivory white. The forms were fine and were originally based on ribbons; later forms consisted mainly of elongated C- and S-shapes; plants, leaves, blossoms, and sometimes shells and small birds were also introduced.

AUSTRIA

The overall effect is glistening and lively.

During the second quarter of the century, the rococo style spread from France to other countries. Francophile German princes eagerly adopted the latest fashions from Paris and often employed French-trained architects and designers. In Austria and Germany, the rococo took a more fanciful and wayward turn, with greater emphasis on forms derived from nature.

Because the baroque style in Austria, Germany, and Italy was already much freer than in France, it needed only a small adjustment to turn baroque decorative forms into rococo ones. This type of rococo found a home both in churches and in palaces.

Germany's other great contribution to the rococo style was the rediscovery (1709-1710) of the Chinese art of porcelain manufacture at Meissen, near Dresden. Meissen achieved enormous popularity; soon, every major court in continental Europe had its own porcelain factory. Small porcelain figures such as those made at Nymphenburg (near Munich) illustrate quintessential rococo style.

Rococo began to decline in the 1760s, denounced by critics who condemned it as tasteless, frivolous, and symbolic of a corrupt society. Within 20 years, it was superseded, together with the baroque, by neo-classicism.

In 1965, Salzburg was the location for the making of the musical "The Sound of Music", directed by Robert Wise and featuring Julie Andrews and Christopher Plummer in the true history of the Von Trapp family.

The Saga of the Von Trapp family (The Sound of Music)

In 1910, Captain Georg von Trapp, a distinguished naval officer in Austria, met Agatha Whitehead. They fell in love, married, and had nine children. When the Austro-Hungarian Empire collapsed at the end of WWI, Captain Von Trapp was relieved from duty. Agatha died suddenly, and he was inconsolable, having lost his wife and his career. Many governesses passed through the house to take care of the children, without success until the appointment of Maria. Maria was teaching at the Benedictine Monastery in Salzburg, and intended to become a nun when she was asked to take over the education of the children. She loved music and helped the Captain to develop their musical education. The children were always musically inclined. They were encouraged by their father, who often accompanied them on guitar, mandolin, or violin. The children formed a group and started to appear at charity or private performances. The Captain's naval stature helped the family forge their careers as musicians, and his name lent a certain air of importance to the group.

The children loved Maria, and the Captain also fell in love. He asked her to marry him, and the marriage took place in 1927. When Captain von Trapp lost his fortune after the Austrian national bank folded, he had nine children to support and no money. For a man in his position, earning a living on the stage was considered déclassé, but they had little choice and started earning money by singing in public. This new life was abruptly halted when

AUSTRIA

Hitler invaded Austria. The Captain asked his family if they wanted to stay or leave. Despite the hardships that they would certainly have to face, they had no moral choice but to depart. They left their home and all of their belongings behind. The grief became almost unbearable when they learned that Himmler himself had taken over their house.

The von Trapp family arrived in America in 1938 and spent the next 18 years on the road. When the Captain died in 1947, the children decided to start families and settle down. All of the children eventually broke away, and the von Trapp family stopped touring in 1956. The family corporation bought an old farm house in Stowe, Vermont, with everyone helping to build the home and take care of the farm. They soon found out that this was not enough to support the whole family, so they resumed touring. While they were away, they rented their home to skiers. This was the beginning of the von Trapp hotel business. Maria died at the age of 82 in 1987 after 30 years spent as a missionary in New Guinea. She rests alongside her husband on their property in Vermont. Rupert, a medical doctor until the mid-1980's, died in 1992 at the age of 82, leaving behind six children and ten grandchildren. Agatha lives near Baltimore, where she helps run a kindergarten. Werner is a dairy farmer with six children and thirteen grandchildren. Hedwig worked at the lodge until his death in 1972. Johanna married in 1948 and had six children; she left the group and lives in Vienna. Martina sang with the group until 1952, when she married; she died in childbirth the same year. Rosmarie lives in Stowe. Lorli (Eleonore) is the mother of seven children; she stopped singing in 1952 and now spends time with her children and ten grandchildren. Johannes received a master's degree in forestry from Yale University and is president of the von Trapp Family Lodge Inc.; he also has two children.

AUSTRIA

INNSBRUCK

Innsbruck, the capital of Tyrol, displays everything Tyrolean, from heel-stomping to thigh-slapping dances and feathered caps. It has a population of 120,000 and was home of the 1964 and 1976 Winter Olympic Games.

Innsbruck is a major rail and road connection: 60% of all north-south traffic between Munich and Rome via the Brenner Pass, and 80 % of all east-west traffic between Vienna and Zurich via the Arlberg tunnel run through the area. Its name is derived from the river Inn and Brücke (bridge).

In the 12th century, the Counts of Tyrol, who then lived in Merano, founded their state on the southern side of the Alps (now Italy).

Two hundred years later, Maximilian I of Habsburg, who later became Emperor, moved the seat of power across the mountain line north to Innsbruck, a place he admired and where he often stayed. Kaiser Max, as the Austrians used to call him, proved to be one of the most cultivated, clever and magnificent rulers of the late 15th century. He was the last knight of the Middle Age, and the first artillery gunner of modern times. He spent a large part of his life at war, aiming to increase his possessions. His arsenal and foundry in Innsbruck were among the largest in Europe. In spite of this, he rarely won a battle, but his alliances by marriage made him one of the first princes in Europe; his grandson Charles V became the most powerful king and emperor of all times. Maximilian married Mary of Burgundy, daughter of Charles the Bold of France and sole heiress to one of the richest countries in Europe. This increased the size of his territories with those of Burgundy and the Netherlands. He married his eldest son, Phillip the Handsome, to the Infant of Spain. Their son, Charles V, inherited all of their possessions. Maximilian used the Habsburg arrogant motto: "A.E.I.O.U." – "Austria Est Imperare Urbi Universo" or "Austria shall rule the world", but, as a modern State ruler, he successfully applied the practice justified by the maxim born in Tyrol: « Others make wars, you, happy Austria, marry! ».

As he was very fond of art, architecture, pageantry and tournaments, his expenditures were enormous and he was constantly nearly bankrupt. After Mary's death in 1482, he married Bianca-Maria Sforza, the rich daughter of the Duke of Milano, probably for the dowry.

Towards the end of his life, he chose Innsbruck as his burial place and commissioned a magnificent mausoleum to be erected in the Palace Chapel. When he came to Innsbruck on his last days, however, the innkeepers closed their gates, exasperated by the unpaid debts left by the noblemen of Maximilian's suite. Disgusted with Innsbruck, the Emperor decided to return to Wien to be buried with his mother in Wiener-Neustadt, where his remains still lie.

Maximilian's Mausoleum was to present 40 statues of the family of Habsburg and other great kings and heroes, 100 small bronze statues of saints and 40 busts of Roman Emperors. At Maximilian's death, it was unfinished; his next of kin completed as much work as they could afford

AUSTRIA

until 1573, when the Church around the Mausoleum was completed. Today, it is surrounded by 28 oversized bronze statues, not only of other prominent Habsburgs but also of various heroes such as King Arthur, Clovis, King of the Franks and Theodoric, King of the Goths. This is the last and the largest existing piece of German Renaissance sculpture.

The church also contains the tomb of Andreas Hofer, the Tyrolean leader of the resistance against the rule of Napoleon, who had him executed.

Another curiosity, the Little Golden Roof, a window roof built in 1500 and covered with 3,400 gilded copper tiles, served as a covered pavilion from which Maximilian could watch knights' tournaments and popular festivals on the square below. The balustrade on the first floor shows the coats of arms of Styria, Austria, Hungary, the Holy Roman Empire, the kingdom of Germany, Philip the Fair, the Sforzas and Tyrol. The second floor balustrade shows on the left side Maximilian facing Bianca Maria Sforza and Mary of Burgundy. On the right side, Maximilian stands between his councilor and his jester.

BRENNER PASS

One of the lowest passes (4,511 feet) through the main chain of the Alps on the Austrian-Italian border, open all year long, the Brenner Pass has been one of the main entrances to Italy from the north since Roman times, and the

EUROPE DIGEST FOR THE HURRIED TOURIST

principal road between the Eastern Alps in Germany and the Po River valley of Italy. Since the 14th century, it has been one of Europe's great trade routes. A carriage road (built in 1772) and railway (completed in 1867) climb steeply from Innsbruck to the Brenner Pass and then descend through the Isarco and Adige river valleys to Verona. The modern Brenner Highway opened in 1970.

FRANCE

FRANCE

METROPOLITAN FRANCE COVERS 211,209 sq mi, the largest area among European Union members. France also has a number of territories in North America (St Peter and Miquelon), the Caribbean (Guadeloupe and Martinique), South America (Guyana), the southern Indian Ocean, the Pacific Ocean, and Antarctica. Metropolitan France extends from the Mediterranean Sea to the English Channel and the North Sea and from the Rhine to the Atlantic Ocean. It is often referred to as L'Hexagone ("The Hexagon") because of the geometric shape of its territory. It is one of the five permanent members of the United Nations Security Council and possesses the third largest number of nuclear weapons in the world as well as the largest number of nuclear power plants in the European Union. The national government of France is divided into executive, legislative, and judicial branches, much like that of the United States. The President shares executive power with his appointee, the Prime Minister. Parliament comprises the National Assembly and the Senate. The independent judiciary is based on a civil law system which evolved from the Napoleonic codes.

THE FRENCH

The French are different: wonderfully different or differently wonderful? That is the question. Many times, one can hear Britons and Americans proclaim with a hiss: "France is OK, but the French!" or "The French are rude, cold, and arrogant"…

This might well seem true at times, as the French do not make much effort to show kindness, especially in Paris. Whatever foreign journalists, especially the British, write about the French, the Americans who come to Paris should remember that the French are the U.S.'s oldest ally. There might be differences from time to time, as happens between friends, but it was the French Treasury and experienced French naval and army leaders that made the difference between the colonists' winning and losing their independence against Britain. True, Americans returned by crossing the Atlantic twice to save France. Today, they are sometimes deceived by the behavior of the French: "Dirty bitches! After all we did for them! Who do they think they are anyway?"

However, the French have always been, and are, generous friends to many Americans, which they are not necessarily to other foreigners.

The French care about being French. They are convinced of their corporate and individual superiority over all

FRANCE

others in the world. Their charm is that they don't despise the rest of the world: they pity them for not being French. On one hand, the cockerel – a colorful bird that makes a great deal of noise, chases off all rivals and lays no eggs – is their national symbol. On the other, Marianne, the symbol of the Republic on coins and stamps, appears with a very thin veil on her body, leaping over the barricades with a musket in hand, and moves the French to tears of real patriotism. Honor is a major part of the French culture.

They are a sensual people: they kiss where others shake hands; they make love in the same way they eat or drink – with gourmandize and refinement. The average Frenchman might well be pictured in the movies as a stout, rather little man with a beret on his head and a baguette under his arm, but he is attracted to all things vibrant, alive, moving, and grandiose. The French see honor in seduction, triumph in a well-cooked entrecote, and world supremacy in a bottle of great Chateau wine. They are public, unabashed people made for special occasions and performances. This is why they are so concerned with appearances. They are at their best in offices, restaurants, opera houses, or on the grand boulevards. They love to feel that life is fast moving, energetic, and stylish. Style is a major concept: cooking, eating, drinking, dressing, making love, going out, vacationing, receiving guests, and going to war, must be done *"comme il faut"* and with style. They respect strict etiquette in public (in private is another thing). They strongly believe in *la règle*, the rule. That is, everything that matters should be done in the right way, in the right place, and at the right time.

EUROPE DIGEST FOR THE HURRIED TOURIST

They ignore petty regulations about parking, pedestrian crossings, smoking, driving, hygiene, and where you may or may not urinate. On anything that matters, they consider themselves experts. Anything on which they are not experts does not matter. Since they are convinced of their superiority, the French are generously prepared to accept that other nations have to exist.

They are far from being politically correct: they are racist, chauvinistic, and xenophobic, though they smile rather than frown at other nations. They see the English, whom they call "roast-beefs" – the English retaliate in calling the French "frogs"– as untrustworthy, small-minded, ridiculous, dressing badly, spending most of their time gardening, playing cricket, and drinking thick, sweet beer in pubs. For almost a century, a permanent hatred has existed between the French and the Germans, which received, and sometimes still are called, a large variety of insulting names : les Boches, Schleuh, Fridolins, Vert-de-Gris, Doryphores, Teutons, Adolf, etc. They no longer hate Germans, but they do not like them. They allow them industrial supremacy and drive Mercedes and BMWs, buy German washing machines, but they feel that Germans have a markedly inferior culture and are ridiculously formal. However, the French have much in common with them: formality, a concept of racial purity, and a belief in an historical destiny. They find that Spanish are proud but noisy, while Swiss and Belgians are objects of merciless satire, and subjects to a million of jokes. The Italians are called macaronis, often despised for their lack of honor (probably after Italy stabbed France in

FRANCE

the back during last world war), but the French love Ferrari, Alfa-Romeo, Italian fashion designers, and Italian food, not to forget, of course, the pizza. There are thousands of pizzerias in France.

Although they seem to despise other cultures, the French are always curious of other ways of life, and foreign products are usually welcome. A third of all the restaurants, shops, and groceries in France are foreign: Vietnamese, Moroccan, Tunisian, Algerian, Chinese (there is an increasing Asiatic population in Paris), Martiniquais, African, Lebanese, Mexican, and American. This feeling of superiority is understandable: the French may no longer own much of the world, but French law, language, and culture persist on every continent – from Canada to the New Hebrides, from Indochina to French Guiana, from the Ivory Coast to Lebanon. Historically, the French have a special relationship with the United States and Canada. They have owned much of the former and populated much of the latter. They admire the Americans for their constitution, their legal system, and the fact that they kicked out the British, but they resent the U.S. invasion in investments, business, film culture, and fast food. They have established a quota system for American films and American music on radio and television channels, restricted the number of fast food outlets, and parked Euro Disney far enough from Paris to give it a sporting chance of failure. Still, Mickey Mouse, MacDonald's, Levi's jeans, Coca Cola, hot-dogs and hamburgers, Harley Davidson, American cigarettes, the wild West cow-boy, rock and pop groups, American movies and crime series, are today an important part of the French culture, especially amongst the youngsters. Anything new in the U.S. will later become fashionable in France.

They love ideas, concepts, and innovations, playing around with things, like democracy, railway systems, and architecture. It is not so much the practical end of the road they're interested in, but the journey itself, the possibilities. They love the latest clothes and gadgets, but they quickly move on to the next trend.

One must understand that the French regard consistency as boring, and to be boring is inexcusable. They are great snobs about their dogs, about where they live, about schools, about where they eat, shop, play tennis, where they take their vacation. One thing that makes this snobbery a little acceptable is that it is generally based on good taste.

France is the country of the four Fs: Food, Fashion, Fragrance, and Frivolity. This is why others often consider the French as inconsistent, and it is true that they seem to act that way. Until recently, they were very reluctant to market economy, but dived happily into some fancy international projects that eventually cost billions to the taxpayer. They have the most beautiful paintings in the world and the ugliest wallpaper. They grow the finest vegetables but never serve them in restaurants. But bear in mind the list of French achievements in the last 70 years:

- one of the finest transatlantic liners,
- the first rear-jet commercial aircraft,

- the Concorde, and the Airbus,
- the Mirage fighter,
- the T.G.V.,
- the N°1 perfume industry,
- the first chip credit card,
- the first pneumatic suspension car,
- their own atomic bomb without any help from outside,
- a space commercial rocket that rivals with NASA,
- the organization "Médecins sans frontières", etc.

They pay 20% more taxes in order to provide childcare, public health insurance, and higher education for all citizens.

Another facet of the French character is their rudeness. They can be awfully rude, especially the Parisians. They are happy to be rude to strangers. While an insult is for life in Great Britain and brings instant fighting in America, the French insult each other dreadfully and then act the next day as if nothing happened. Among friends, insults can be exchanged without any permanent damage to the relationship. They very seldom come to real fighting. The exchange consists of names and words (body parts, birds or animals, and other swearwords), shouted at each other with a lot of melodramatic grimaces and ugly gestures: the first one short of vocabulary bows down. The best place to experiment it is to take a cab during rush hour.

SHOPS

The French have the largest supermarkets in the world outside of America, but they also have innumerable specialized shops. For instance, *boulangeries* sell only bread, and *poissonneries* sell only fish. Pharmacies sell only drugs.

Other shop names to remember are:

- *Boucheries*, selling meat;
- *Charcuteries*, selling cooked meat;
- *Fromageries*, selling cheese (fromages);
- *Patisseries*, bakeries, usually associated with boulangeries;
- *Laveries* : Laundromats
- *Epiceries* (from the word *épices*, spices): small shops carrying all kinds of goods.

All these shops are closed on Sundays, except for boulangeries/patisseries, and those run by Muslims, which close on Friday. These last ones are usually open until late in the evening.

HYGIENE

The French have a saying: "Don't be afraid of the microbes." The use of soap is one of the lowest in Western Europe. Until quite recently, the bidet was currently replacing a shower and, still in the 60s, 40% of the flats in Paris did not have a bathroom. Today, things have greatly progressed. All rest rooms in public places provide toilet paper (in the 50s, very often only newspapers or wrapping paper would be found), and Turkish toilets have practically disappeared. According to an official survey, the French wash and brush their teeth 14 times per week, which is less than the Italians, who brush 19 times. There is some progress though: in 2007, the French bought 1.7 toothbrushes per head, up from 1.3 in 2002. And it has been calculated that the French housewife spends an average of 1.10 hour per day cleaning her house, which is the highest figure in Europe.

LANGUAGE

After the Gallo-Roman era and the barbaric invasions, each region of the present territory had its own language. Kings of France fought to conquer the land and unify the dialects to French. Today, France fights to preserve its language. The Académie Française works to ensure its purity. They examine every new word appearing on the streets or from abroad and decide when it is appropriate to include it in the Academy Dictionary. It is needless to say that the work is never completed. And if hundreds of foreign words have become part of the French language, French have also provided many words to the world, including tête-à-tête, rendezvous, sabotage, maneuvers, espionage, liaison, coup d'état, carte-blanche, faux pas, and scores more, especially terms used in cuisine.

ETIQUETTE

In France, one eats at the table with the hands rested both side of your plate (who knows what your hands could be at if under the table?) and one uses left hand for fork and right hand for knife together. Foreigners often fail to appreciate the formal code of greeting in France. The French consider it rude to use first names with a new acquaintance too soon. It requires a little time and the question: "May I call you X...?" In business, this process is faster but takes longer in formal settings.

SIX CODES OF BEHAVIOR:[1]

1. Don't smile! The French do not smile at strangers. They do not smile without a reason. This is called *une mine d'enterrement*, (a funeral expression.) They will not understand if you smile when your eyes meet, or they might take it as an attempt at flirtation. Philippe Labro, a well-known figure in journalism and television, tells how, when he was studying at the University of Virginia, he was summoned before the Student Council and reprimanded for not smiling when he was running into people on the campus. On the contrary, you are welcome to smile at someone if you find both of you in a funny or awkward situation.

2. Flirt! (with the opposite sex of course...)

---

[1] French or Foe? by Polly Platt – Culture Crossings Ltd London

FRANCE

3. Use the ten magic words.

    Stage A: (five magic words): "*Excusez-moi de vous déranger, Monsieur (Madame)*": Sorry to bother you, Mr. (Mrs.). Approached with this code, the Frenchman is reassured the intruder knows how to behave, and understands that this is a helpless, harmless brand of foreigner.

    Stage B: (Five magic words): "*mais j'ai un problème*" I have a problem. A variant is: "excuse me, do you think it would be possible..." with a little pathos when expressing your wishes: instead of saying: « Barman, one Martini! », saying « Monsieur, if it is possible, I would very much like a Martini » will bring you better service and courtesy.

4. Add Monsieur or Madame to *Bonjour* and *Au revoir* when entering or exiting. You will get better attention if you say "Monsieur" to a shopkeeper or a waiter ("Mademoiselle" for a girl, "Madame" if she's obviously not a Mademoiselle any more). At work, if behind the scenes, jacquets are off, ties undone, and a *Gauloise* hangs from the mouth, on the front scene, etiquette dictates that company members call each other "Monsieur W" or "Madame Y." "*S'il vous plait*" is also important in the exchanges between guest and service. Remember: the French are sensitive and often touchy about respect. You

have to seduce them.

5. Shake hands: The French shake hands with everyone, but it is important to remember with whom one has shaken hands on a given day. It is bad manners to shake hands twice. Every morning, French business colleagues shake hands with each other. Everything has to be proper before anyone goes to work, whatever time it takes.

The happy bottom line is that, even being a foreigner at sea in a new culture, if you are in harmony with the codes, the French will be astoundingly aware and understanding of your anxieties and the complications of your life.

FOOD AND DRINK

This is an important matter as France is generally recognized as the Mecca of gastronomy. Food and cooking are topics of conversation. This section gives a few principles about eating. A chapter further down is consecrated to the places favored by local customers, where French cuisine can be appreciated at its best, and introduce some traditional Provencal dishes that one should definitely not miss (see the chapter on Provence).

Enjoyment of food at a good restaurant or in a gourmet's home is almost a spiritual experience. Eating is a ritual, although one that has been somewhat shattered by fast food, kebab stands, and sandwich bars, mostly among youngsters and office workers. Outside of Paris and the largest cities, there are still many places where two hours are allowed for lunch. In many small towns, you will lose your temper at finding everything closed between 12 and 2 pm, except of course restaurants. Slowly, however, this habit tends to disappear as more and more people are opting for a shorter lunch break in order to leave work early. The difference between a good restaurant and a bad one can be cosmic, between a cheap restaurant and an expensive one, even more. Maximum expenditure has no limit.

Count on a minimum of 20 to 30 € for a reasonable meal with drinks (excluding bottled wines; look for cheaper carafe wine, if available). The question is to find the decent restaurant at the minimum price. Here is how to find a place to eat: look at the menu-card outside, and focus on prices that can be compared from one restaurant to the other, for instance, "oeuf mayonnaise" (hardboiled egg with mayonnaise), 5 to 7 €, tomato mozzarella, 8 to 10 €, pizza, 8 to 10 €, or entrecote, 15 to 20 €. The price level is an indication of fair food. Cheaper might mean bad quality, but more expensive is not necessarily better. Then look inside and see how many tables are empty. If more than three are empty at busy hours (usually between 12.30PM and 2PM), avoid it. If customers line up at the entrance, this is a definite sign that the place is good and inexpensive.

SERVICE CHARGES AND TIPS

In more than half of the cases, the French waiter will show annoyance and irritation to be disturbed by the customer. True enough, the job is difficult, but sometimes their grim face and attitude are too much. Polly Platt's method, cited here above, could bring enlightenment. Service charges are always included in the bill, but the usage is to leave some kind of a tip. If totally satisfied by personalized friendly and swift service, a tip of up to 10% might be satisfactory. As for bad service, I have an anecdote: a customer in a big restaurant on the Champs-Elysees, being totally disgusted by the food served and the waiter's attitude, made a loud scandal and required from the cashier a refund of the included service charge (which was accommodated). Check the bill. Beware of the "sub-marine" method: when the change comes back in the saucer, the bills might be put above the returned check. If the customer picks-up the bills and leaves the check on the saucer, any coins lying hidden under the check would also be left behind.

FRANCE

PARIS

WHEN ARRIVING AT the hotel in Paris, ask at the reception desk for a free map of the city. It is usually available at all good hotels and provides a map of the metro/and bus networks. It will help to locate the monuments, museums, and restaurants.

City of Love? City of Light? City of Thought? City of Art and Beauty?

Today, Paris looks clean. From the 18th to 20th century, mostly due to coal central heating, buildings gradually acquired a dark, stained appearance. At the beginning of the 1960s, André Malraux, then Minister of Cultural Affairs, issued a decree that all facades should be cleaned or repainted. Consequently, Paris recovered its original look.

Public transportation is clean (mostly), fast (except for buses trapped in traffic jams), reliable (except when on strike, which is quite often), and comfortable (except at rush hours). Streets are washed down regularly; special motorbikes with vacuum cleaning devices try to clean all of the dogs' souvenirs from the sidewalks. Be careful though – in Paris it is better to walk looking down.

Within its administrative limits, which remain unchanged since 1860, the city of Paris has an estimated population of 2.2 million. The Paris metropolitan area has a population of 11.8 million.

Paris boundaries are delimited by the Boulevards des Maréchaux, which were built on the former fortified walls surrounding Paris, demolished after 1920, and bear the names of Napoléon's field marshals.

The Paris region receives 45 million tourists annually, 60% of whom are foreign visitors. The Eiffel Tower, by far the most famous monument, averages over 6 million visitors per year and more than 200 million since its construction. Disneyland Paris is a major tourist attraction, not only for visitors to Paris but for visitors to the rest of Europe as well, with 14.5 million visitors in 2007.

HISTORICAL BACKGROUND

The Gallic tribe, called the Parisii, lived on an island on the Seine around 250 B.C. Their town was called Lucotetium. After the Roman general Labenius defeated the Gauls in 52 B.C., a Roman town was erected there. In the 5th century AD, Attila and his Huns invaded Gaul but were stopped before reaching Paris, assumedly by Saint Genevieve's prayers: she was the first of a series of French heroines including Joan of Arc, Jeanne Hachette, Sarah Bernhardt, Marie Curie, Mata Hari, and Brigitte Bardot. In the 6th century, Clovis defeated the last Roman army, was crowned king of the Franks in 508, and chose Paris as the capital. Charlemagne, Charles the Great, king of the Franks founded the Holy Roman Empire, the first representation of a united Europe. The first king to be crowned king of France was Hugh Capet. The Capetians ruled France until the beheading of Louis XVI in 1792. Except for Rome, Paris has seen more fighting, wars, invasions, uprisings, and revolutions than any other city in the world.

The Parisians have always been, and still are considered

FRANCE

as independent, versatile, and buoyant people. Protesting and rioting are a Parisian hobby as the long but non exhaustive list hereafter shows:

- 12th c.: Students refuse the control of the church and immigrate to the Left Bank;
- 1355: Insurrection of Merchants; Paris proclaims itself an independent commune;
- 15th c.: Paris alliance with the English during the One Hundred Years war;
- Late 16th c.: The Saint Barthelemy massacre of Protestants;
- 1648- 1649: Uprising of the Parliament against the Regent mother of Louis XIV;
- 1650- 1653: Uprising of the nobility, who make a coalition with the Parliament;
- 1789: The French Revolution, started in Paris;
- 1830: Overthrow of King Charles X;
- 1848: Overthrow of King Louis-Philippe;
- 1871: The Commune;
- 1934: Overthrow of the Prime Minister by a nationalist mob;
- 1944: Rising of Paris against the Germans;
- 1968: Student revolution; and many other protests.

The government has always feared and still fears these movements. In fact, when the Paris Prefect Haussmann proposed the new town planning of Paris in 1853, he was backed by Napoleon III, who found the large and straight avenues to be very convenient for marching troops and deploying artillery against the demonstrators.

Nowadays, with the tolerance adopted by the successive governments after 1980, the so-called "suburban culture" is prevailing. It seems that being rude is modern behavior. Arrogant service in restaurants, complete lack of politeness and disrespect seem to be the signs of this new culture.

Is Paris the Most Beautiful City In The World? Some contest this assertion, but when you have visited Paris, or lived in it, you always conclude that Paris is, if not the most beautiful, certainly the most attractive. Paris has more bridges, monuments, restaurants, theaters, and concert halls than any other city in the world.

Sure, other capitals have highlights, but none offers so much to see and so many different faces as Paris.

PARIS DISTRICTS

Since 1860, when bordering communes were annexed to the city, the administrative map of Paris has comprised 20 municipal *arrondissements* (districts), numbered 1 to 20 (I to XX), which run in a clockwise spiral outward from its most central, the first arrondissement.

The River Seine, flowing from east to west, divides Paris. The Right Bank (north side) contains the business, financial, press, and fashion districts as well as The Louvre museum and The Presidential Palace. The Left Bank (south side) contains the Parliament Houses, universities and student residences, art galleries, and the Latin Quarter.

FRANCE

Main districts

- **Place de la Bastille** (4th, 11th, and 12th arrondissements, Right Bank) is a district of great historical significance. On July 14, 1789, the Bastille Fortress was assaulted and taken by Paris revolutionaries. Because of its symbolic value, the square is often a site for political demonstrations.

- **Champs-Élysées** (8th arrondissement, Right Bank) is one of the most famous streets in the world. It is 210 feet wide and runs 1.25 miles from the Arc of Triumph to the Place de la Concorde. This prestigious avenue is lined with cinemas, top fashion shops, restaurants, airlines offices, international business companies, and car manufacturers, which pay rents as high as $1.5 million per 1,000 square feet, making the avenue the second most expensive strip of real estate in Europe (London's Bond Street ranked first in 2010). It retrieved the unfortunate first rank in 2011.

- **Place de la Concorde** (8th arrondissement, Right Bank) is at the foot of the Champs-Élysées. Formerly built as the Place Louis XV, it was the site of the infamous guillotine during the Revolutionary period. The Egyptian obelisk is Paris' oldest monument. On either side of the Rue Royale, there are two identical stone buildings: the eastern one houses the French Naval Ministry; the western, the luxurious Hôtel de Crillon. Nearby, Place Vendôme is famous for its fashionable and deluxe hotels (Hôtel Ritz and Hôtel de Vendôme) and its jewelers. Many famous fashion designers have their headquarters in the square and the adjacent Rue de la Paix. Coco Chanel was permanently residing at Hotel Ritz. Place Vendôme and Rue de la Paix are also the seat of 24 of the world's greatest jewelers, such as Van Cleef & Arpels, Chopard, Cartier, Boucheron, and others.

• **Les Halles** (1st arrondissement, Right Bank) was formerly Paris' central meat and food products market and, since the late 1970s, a major shopping centre around an important metro connection station (Châtelet-Les Halles, the biggest in Europe). The past iron cast and glass halls, built between 1952 and 1870, were destroyed in 1971, much to the dismay of Paris lovers, and were replaced by the Forum des Halles. The central market of Paris, the biggest wholesale food market in the world, was transferred to Rungis, in the southern suburbs.

• **Le Marais** (3rd and 4th arrondissements) is a trendy Right Bank district. It is architecturally well preserved, and some of the oldest houses and buildings of Paris can be found there. It is a very culturally open place.

• **Avenue Montaigne** (8th arrondissement, Right Bank), next to the Champs-Élysées, is home to luxury brand labels such as Chanel, Louis Vuitton, Dior, and Givenchy.

• **Montmartre** (18th arrondissement, Right Bank) is a historic area on the Butte Montmartre, home to the Basilique du Sacré-Cœur. Montmartre has always had a history with artists (see hereunder).

• **Montparnasse** (14th arrondissement) is a historic Left Bank area famous for artists' studios, music halls, and cafés. The large Montparnasse– Bienvenue métro station and the lone Tour Montparnasse skyscraper are located there.

• **Avenue de l'Opéra** (9th arrondissement, Right Bank) is the area around the Opéra Garnier and the capital's densest concentration of department stores and offices. A few examples are the Printemps and Galeries Lafayette department stores and the Paris headquarters of Crédit Lyonnais and American Express.

•**Quartier Latin** (5th and 6th arrondissements, Left Bank) is a 12th-century scholastic center, known for its lively atmosphere and its numerous bistros. Various higher-education establishments, such as the École Normale Supérieure, the Sorbonne, the Faculties of Law and Medicine, make it a major educational centre in Paris.

•**Faubourg Saint-Honoré** (8th arrondissement, Right Bank) is one of Paris' high-fashion districts, home to labels such as Hermès and Christian Lacroix.

The best way to visit Paris is to use public transportation during the day, as taxicabs are difficult to get during rush hours and expensive. However, they should be preferred at night.

RATP (the public transportation system) operates 654 bus lines, which are the best way to see Paris, and the Metro, Paris' most important transportation system.

Métro (for Metropolitan)

The system boasts 131 miles of track and 16 lines with 298 stations (not including RER stations), 87 of these offering connections between lines. It is said that every building in Paris is within 500 meters (3/10 mile) of a métro station. Roughly, 6 million people per day patronize the métro, which employs over 15,000. This tight network allows easy access to any place in Paris.

EUROPE DIGEST FOR THE HURRIED TOURIST

RER (Réseau Express Régional – Regional express network) is a rapid transit system serving Paris and its suburbs. It is fully interconnected with the Métro, as well as with SNCF (French national railways).

Finding your way in Métro is simple: direction signs are abundant and easily followed. Every station offers a big plan of the network outside the entrance and several inside. Lines are color-coded and numbered, and are also named according to the city gate – or *porte* – at the end of the line. For example, Line 4 running to the north will be indicated as going in the direction of Porte de Clignancourt, while southbound would be Porte d'Orléans.

The busiest stations offer express computerized route finders: at the touch of a button, you'll be shown four alternative routes to your selected destination, on foot or by public transport.

Tickets are valid on the entire RATP network: metro, bus, tram, and RER (regional express network) on its inner city course.

Single tickets (€1.60) may be purchased at the station counters (fr. guichets) each time, but the better value is a carnet of 10 (adults: €11.40; children ages 4-9: €5.70), which will save you queuing. Ticket books (and certain passes) may also be purchased from a network of 1,500 retailers approved by RATP – including bookstores, newsstands, and tobacconists. Tickets are valid for one single trip on the Métro, or bus.

"T+" tickets cost slightly more (€1.70 single and €12.00 a book of ten) and offer the possibility to unlimited connections bus to bus within a 90-minute period. If you chose to use mainly buses, and change from one line to another, the T+ ticket will prove a good deal.

Passes are also available: At a cost of € 5.90 for inner Paris, One-day Mobilis passes are valid on the métro, buses, RER trains, and the Montmartre funicular – but cannot be used for travel to, or from, CDG and Orly airports. An advantage of this pass, when compared to paper tickets, is that transfers between bus and rail lines do not require a new fare. The pass may be purchased in advance at station counters; its day of validity starts upon the first use, and ends at around 12:45 or 1:00 a.m. the following morning, when Métro service stops.

Paris Visit Pass is a special pass offered only to foreign travelers. It provides several advantages over the one-day Mobilis pass: it is valid for either 1, 2, 3 or 5 days' unlimited use on the entire RATP network: métro, RER, day & night buses, trams, the Montmartre funicular, and SNCF suburban trains. It also privileges including 20-50% discounts on admission to 18 popular tourist attractions in and near Paris – such as 20% off on tickets to Disneyland, 50% off at the Lido cabaret, a free shopping bag plus 10% off on purchases at Galeries Lafayette.

Paris Visite pass can be purchased in all Paris Metro, RER, bus terminal ticket counters, RATP Boutiques, RATP sales desks at Orly and CDG airports and Paris tourist offices. You can also buy your pass in certain travel agencies and tour operators abroad, or online, in advance of your trip to Paris, and activate it on any day of the week you choose.

EUROPE DIGEST FOR THE HURRIED TOURIST

Type Google "Paris visit pass" for web connection with various resellers.

Buses

Wherever your hotel or hostel is located, you might find that there's a bus stop that's closer to where you're sleeping than the nearest Metro station. Buses are above ground as opposed to the Metro or RER, and will show you more of the city. You'll watch monuments go by and have a better idea of where you are when you get off. Moreover, if you get a good seat with a view, you could even use a trip on a Paris bus as an unguided city tour.

The following link will lead to a printable Paris bus map that can be printed in advance, or loaded on your smartphone.

parispages.com/Metro/gifs/bus.pdf

Taxis

17,200 taxis operate in Paris, day and night. This is much less than in London and explains the difficulty of finding one at rush hour. Unfortunately, the taxi corporation keeps blocking any attempt to increase the number of licenses.

Anyone claiming to be a taxi driver who does not have a specially equipped vehicle is illegal. This equipment includes the illuminated "Taxi Parisien" sign on the roof, a display meter showing the cost of the journey, a display at the rear of the vehicle visible from the exterior showing the daily duration of use of the vehicle, and a plate fixed to the front right-hand wing of the vehicle bearing the license number.

FRANCE

You can take a taxi by hailing one on the street (it is unoccupied if the sign on the roof is green), at a taxi stand, or by calling one of the main taxi operators. When calling a taxi through a radio connection, be aware that the approach time will be charged. It can be up to 20 minutes. It is better to use the new central number: 01 45 30 30 30, which re-connects you with the nearest taxi stand. This shortens the approach time.

Tariffs are a bit complicated. The meter operates increasingly on three modes (the ABC letters are shown on the meter, which is operated by hand):

Tariff A: Monday to Saturday, inside Paris, from 10.00 to 17.00

Tariff B: Weekdays from 07.00 to 10.00, 17.00 to 19.00, Sunday 07.00 to 24.00 and outer Paris (beginning at circle Boulevards) from 07.00 to 19.00

Tariff C: Inner Paris everyday 00.00 to 07.00, outer Paris 19.00 to 07.00

Generally, taxi drivers are honest and reliable. However, it is recommended to check the meter during the trip and see that the meter is switched accordingly to the tariffs above. Though the price indicated by the meter is net, there might be a small surcharge for large pieces of luggage, and drivers expect a tip (only if the client is satisfied). If one knows Paris well, one can ask the driver to take a particular route. It is always good to ask for a receipt before paying, on which are the name and address of the taxi company and where to complain in case of litigation. This will avoid any possible problems.

EUROPE DIGEST FOR THE HURRIED TOURIST

These simple rules apply to taxis everywhere in Europe, but especially in France and in Italy.

AMERICANS IN PARIS

In the first 40 years of the 20th century, many Americans, attracted by the beauty and the atmosphere of Paris, came over and many settled there. Mingling with French writers like Colette, Anatole France, Guillaume Apollinaire, Paul Claudel, and Louis Aragon; surrealist painters such as Picasso, Matisse, Chagall, and Modigliani; musicians like Strawinsky and Prokofiev as well as with the French and international aristocracy looking for exotic intellectual entertainment, they contributed to making the Left Bank into a place of literary and artistic development. One of the leaders of this group of artists and writers was Gertrude Stein, who came to live in Paris in 1903. At the end of the World War I, American servicemen willing to postpone their return to the U.S. were allowed to study at European schools. So did John Dos Passos, who attended classes at the Sorbonne.

In 1919, Sylvia Beach, who was studying French Literature at the Sorbonne, decided to open the Shakespeare & Company bookstore, which became one of main gathering places for all English-speaking residents of Paris. The shop was located near the Odeon Theatre. One of the first visitors was James Joyce, who spent a lot of his time there. He completed "Ulysses" in Paris, which was published by Beach in 1922. Other visitors and friends included Ezra Pound, Man Ray, John dos Passos, Josephine Baker,

Hemingway, F. Scott Fitzgerald, Henry Miller, Paul Elliot, and many others who were living on the Left Bank. In 1940, it remained opened until America entered the war. Under the threat that the Germans would confiscate all books, Sylvia Beach closed Shakespeare and Company forever.

In 1964, another American, George Whitman, opened the present Shakespeare and Company on the square along the Quai de Montebello, where it remains today. He somehow recreated a very peculiar and attractive atmosphere, making this is a place to visit. Another famous resident was Helena Rubenstein, who lived in Paris from 1930 until May 1940, when she and her husband sailed hurriedly back to the U.S. just before the Germans arrived.

Isadora Duncan lived at 5 rue Danton and led a school of dance.

Alexander Calder lived in Paris for several years, visiting with his friends Léger, Miro, and Jean Cocteau.

Cole Porter and his wife stayed at 13 rue Monsieur from 1919 to 1939. He was at the piano in 1924 for the first audition in Paris of Gershwin's "Rhapsody in Blue." George Gershwin stayed in a hotel on the Right Bank in 1928 while composing "An American in Paris."

WHAT TO SEE AND DO IN PARIS

If you plan to visit one or several museums or monuments during your stay in Paris, it is highly recommended to purchase entrance tickets in advance on Internet. Huge lines form in the summer, and the waiting time can be up to two or three hours. With a ticket bought in advance, you have priority access, saving time and the hustle.

All museums and monuments have their own Web site and allow for buying tickets in advance. Some offer to send the tickets by mail, or to pick them up at withdrawal points (the Louvre, for instance), or receive an e-ticket for printing at home.

If planning to visit only one or two places, try the museum's or monument's Web site, or ticketweb.com, and ticketnet.fr. If planning to visit several monuments, the suggestion is to purchase a museum pass from paris-museumpass.com. Also, be sure to consult the sites for opening times and days.

Practically everywhere, special prices are granted for groups and children under 18.

Apart from temporary exhibitions and galleries, there are more than 80 permanent museums in Paris. Here is a short listing of those not to miss:

MUSEE DU LOUVRE
Métro: Palais Royal – Musée du Louvre
louvre.fr
Perhaps the biggest museum in the world, along with the British Museum in London, this ex-royal palace houses hundreds of thousands of objects and works of art from Antiquity until the 19th century, including the Mona Lisa, the Venus de Milo, and others.

FRANCE

MUSEE D'ORSAY
Métro: Concorde or Solférino
musee-orsay.fr
Located in the 19th century former Orsay Railway station, this museum is oriented towards Impressionism and its related styles.

MUSEE NATIONAL PICASSO
Métro: Saint-Paul
This museum contains 203 paintings, 191 sculptures, 85 ceramics, and over 3s drawings, engravings, and manuscripts by Picasso. Besides this personal collection, the museum also has some works of Cézanne and Matisse.

MUSEE GREVIN (WAX MUSEUM)
Métro: Richelieu Drouot – Rue Montmartre
An equivalent to Madame Tussaud's wax museum in London, the Musée Grévin presents some 450 wax figures, arranged in about fifty striking scenes to bring to life the highlights of French history, as well as today's sport and show-business celebrities.

MUSEE MARMOTTAN
Métro: La Muette
The Musée Marmottan is housed in a 19th century mansion in the fashionable Auteuil Western district of Paris on the edge of the Bois de Boulogne. It contains the best permanent collection of impressionist paintings by Claude Monet, Renoir, Berthe Morissot, Manet, Degas, Pissarro,

Gauguin, Sisley, and others.

CENTRE POMPIDOU
Métro: Châtelet - Hôtel de Ville - Rambuteau This modern-style building, nicknamed *L'usine à gaz* (gas works), houses the Modern Art National Museum and hosts a vast library, movies, shows, and concerts.

OTHER POINTS OF INTEREST

EIFFEL TOWER
tour-eiffel.fr

This spectacular 300m high metal tower was built in 1889 to commemorate the centenary of the French Revolution and is a famous icon of Paris. You can visit any of the three floors (the first is at 57 m, the second at 115 m, and the third at 276 m) which can be accessed by elevator or stairs. The top of the aerial is 320 m above the ground; on a nice day, you can see all of Paris. The top level is only accessible by elevator, with long lines in peak season, so start early.

CRUISES ON THE SEINE RIVER
Several companies operate cruises commented in different languages. Boats leave from the Port de la Bourdonnais near the Eiffel Tower or from the wharf alongside Notre Dame Cathedral.

It is an unforgettable experience. As in London, enjoying a trip on the river is a must. This is the best way to see the major monuments and the bridges of Paris with a panoramic view. At night, the enchantment of these monuments floodlighted is simply overwhelming.

bateauxparisiens.com
vedettesdupontneuf.fr
vedettesdeparis.com

The Batobus is a regular boat line with stops at the Eiffel Tower, Musée d'Orsay, Saint Germain-des-Prés, Notre Dame, Hôtel-de-Ville, and the Louvre.

NOTRE-DAME CATHEDRAL
6, place du Parvis Notre Dame, Ile de la Cité, 75004 Paris.

Métro: Cité or St-Michel.

cathedraledeparis.com

"Each face, each stone of this venerable monument is not only a page of the history of the country, but also of the history of knowledge and art....

Time is the architect, the people are the builder."

Victor Hugo, Notre-Dame de Paris

The Gothic majesty of Notre-Dame dominates the Seine and the Ile-de-la-Cité. Although construction started in 1163, it was not completed until roughly 180 years later in about 1345.

For a look at the upper parts of the church, the Seine River, and much of Paris, climb the 387 steps to the top of one of the towers.

Six masses are celebrated on Sunday, four on weekdays

and one on Saturday. Morning Prayer is held on Sundays at 9:30AM. Evensong takes place Monday through Friday from 5:45PM to 6:10PM and Sundays at 5:30PM.

MARCHE AUX PUCES

This is the largest flea market in the world. Open Saturday, Sunday, and Monday. Métro: Porte de Clignancourt.

Les Puces (fleas), as the Parisians call it, cover 18 acres, and receive approximately 180,000 visitors each weekend.

It is easy to find: from Porte de Clignancourt, follow the crowd. The market begins after passing under the Ring Motorway (Boulevard Périphérique). It is one of these places where you will really feel the pulse of Paris. Leave your passport in the hotel's safe, hide your wallet under your shirt, and do not carry a big amount of money – practically all merchants accept credit cards.

PARIS HELICOPTER

A helicopter ride provides a costly but unforgettable air trip above Paris.

heliparis.com or helifrance.fr

LITERARY PROMENADE

This walking tour of the Left Bank features an actor telling the story of writers in Paris. Duration 1-1/2 hrs. Daily at 2:30PM and 7:30PM from the steps of the Odeon Theater. Tél : 0148078072, cell phone: 0603277352

FRANCE

CABARET LIDO
116, Champs-Elysées, Paris VIII Tel.01 40 76 56 10
lido.fr/English
This music hall features an international perfectly staged show, with 70 dancers including the famous Blue bell girls.

MOULIN ROUGE
82, Boulevard de Clichy, Paris XVIII Tel. 01 53 09 82 82
Métro: Blanche
moulinrouge.fr
This is where the French Can Can was born. The painter Toulouse-Lautrec used to frequent the Moulin Rouge at the end of 19th century. Nicole Kidman refreshed this favorite Parisian music-hall with her film "Moulin Rouge", directed by Baz Luhrmann in 2001.

CRAZY HORSE
lecrazyhorseparis.com
The show is a sophisticated celebration of the female form. Trained in ballet, all the dancers are perfectly integrated into the full choreography of the piece, creating the most stunning possible visual effect through their movements and bodies.

HARRY'S BAR
5 rue Daunou (near the Opera). After the liberation of Paris, to reach the bar, the G.I.s used to say to the taxi driver: "Sank roo donoo, please!" Open since 1915, this

EUROPE DIGEST FOR THE HURRIED TOURIST

NewYork style bar has invented some of the world's most famous cocktails such as the White Lady in 1919, the Bloody Mary in 1921, the Sidecar in 1931, and many others. Harry's Bar has welcomed many preeminent patrons such as Ernest Hemingway, George Gerschwin, Franklin D. Roosevelt, Burt Lancaster and others. It is also the home of the International Bar Flies Association.

RUE MOUFFETARD
A typical and lively market street on the Left Bank.

SHAKESPEARE & CO
The English bookstore in front of Notre-Dame on the Left Bank features heaps of books. Its narrow staircase to the first floor, its small rooms, and corridors give it a very peculiar and attractive atmosphere.

STROLLING ALONG THE BOUQUINISTES ON THE SEINE'S WATERFRONT.
Bouquinistes (French term for secondhand bookstores) can be considered a landmark of Paris. There are nearly 250 of them, mainly located near the Cathedral Notre-Dame of Paris, alongside the banks of the Seine River. Old books, papers, posters, postcards, and maps can be found there – and perhaps, who knows, the exceptional discovery of a real antique document.

MONTMARTRE
Montmartre is a hill (*la butte Montmartre*) which is 130

m high, giving its name to the surrounding district.

Montmartre is primarily known for the white-domed Basilica of the Sacré Cœur, on its summit, and as a nightclub district. Many artists, including Salvador Dalí, Modigliani, Claude Monet, Pablo Picasso, and Vincent van Gogh, had studios in or worked around Montmartre. Montmartre was also the setting for several films, including "Moulin Rouge" in 2001.

From the steps in front of the Basilica, one has a breathtaking aerial view of Paris. Nearby, the Place du Tertre offers a wide choice of restaurants displaying their tables and colorful umbrellas amid artists who set up their easels each day of the week. A funicular railway ascends the hill from the south side. Access with one Métro ticket, or card.

The Paris Travel Club (paristravelclub.com) can provide you with exclusive reservations at reduced rates, or private guided assistance in more than 200 opportunities such as cabaret shows, monuments or museums visits, food and wine experiences, or individual shopping tours.

WHERE TO EAT IN PARIS

When in Paris, if you have a (very) comfortable bank account, dine at least once at a one-, two-, or three- "*macarons*" (stars) restaurant as graded by the Red Michelin Guide, the French Bible in Gastronomy. Each year, scores of Michelin inspectors, always strictly incognito, visit a large majority of the hotels and restaurants all around France. It is a token of quality just to be nominated in the book. There is fierce competition to be upgraded with the famous macarons, of which only a limited number are awarded. The owners make large efforts to acquire this label. To be degraded turns sometimes to dramatic situations, such as was the suicide in 2003 of the great chef Bernard Loiseau when he underwent critics and lost his three macarons status.

Quite understandingly, building notoriety leads to heavy investments, and the prices can accordingly rise to stratospheric heights, particularly if one orders a top ranked bottle of wine.

If you really decide to have this luxurious but costly experience, here are a few suggestions (addresses to be found in the Red Michelin Guide – prices are indicated for the year 2010 and do usually not include wines). In all places, jacket and tie are recommended.

Le Jules Verne (second floor of the Eiffel Tower)
Métro: Bir-Hakeim Tel. 01 45 55 61 44
lejulesverne-paris.com
It offers great food, beautiful decoration, and magical view over Paris.
Lunch menu weekdays 85€, à la carte 145/240€.

L'Espadon (in the Hotel Ritz)
Place Vendôme, Paris I Métro : Opéra Tel. 01 44 58 10 55
ritzparis.com
Weekdays lunch menu 70€, à la carte 165/250€

FRANCE

"Dining at the Ritz in Paris"…this is certainly one of those souvenirs one cannot forget!

When at the Ritz, you can also prefer the Bar Vendôme, which serves light lunches at a more affordable price.

La Tour d'Argent
15, Quai Tournelle Paris V Métro Pont-Marie Tel. 01 43 54 23 31
latourdargent.com

On the 6th floor above the Seine River and in front of Notre-Dame. –Try to reserreserve one of the tables by the windows in front of Notre-Dame (the utmost are the tables numbered 001, 002, and 003) or nothing. Its worldwide famous specialty, the "Caneton Tour d'Argent" is priced 130€ (for two), there is a lunch menu at 65€, à la carte 250/300€

Taillevent (near the Arch of Triumph).
15, rue Lamennais Paris VIII Métro: Charles de Gaulle
Tel. 01 44 4 95 15 01
taillevent.com

Discreet and elegant, this is a favorite of businesspeople.

Lunch menu 80€ (a special offer at 95€ includes drinks), card 130/225€

Alain Ducasse in Plaza Athenée (in the 5 * Plaza Athenée Hotel
25, Avenue Montaigne Métro: Alma-Marceau Tel. 01 53 67 66 02
alain-ducasse.com

Featuring sumptuous décor and inventive cuisine by Alain Ducasse, one of the world's top chefs, this restaurant in one of the top hotels in Paris is granted with three Michelin stars.

But this must be paid for: cheapest Menus are at 85 €, and count 300 € à la carte (if careful in choice).

La Grande Cascade (Bois de Boulogne)
Allée de Longchamp Paris XVI Tel. 01 45 27 33 51
grandecascade.com

A charming 1850 pavilion with a rotunda and a large terrace situated in the heart of the Bois de Boulogne, 15 minutes from the Arch of Triumph. A delightful place, especially on a sunny day.

Menus 85 (wine and coffee included)/210€, à la carte 127/207€

Apart from these summits of French Cuisine, there are scores of excellent and more affordable restaurants. Here again, I would recommend to consult the Red Michelin book and read their comments and indication of prices.

THE CAFÉS

The hurried traveler can always grab a sandwich or a snack at one of the hundreds of cafés in Paris, which are to be found at practically one street-corner out of ten, sometimes two or three facing each other.

A café once primarily served coffee. Today, it can serve coffee and drinks, including wines and spirits, and light food including sandwiches like the great variation of fillings in a French *baguette*, "Croque-monsieur" (hot ham and cheese grilled sandwich), more exotic Italian Bruschetta (grilled bread with various toppings), or Kebabs (sliced grilled meat of lamb or chicken with salad, wrapped in a thin loaf of bread). The favorite sandwich in France remains the *jambon-beurre*, cooked ham and butter on a baguette, 1.2 billion of which were sold last year.

Many cafés offer seated areas and an open-air terrace on the sidewalk, but one can have food and drinks standing at the bar.

This is the cheapest alternative for a quick snack, definitely "French".

The cafés exist also in Italy, Belgium, and Switzerland.

For a more consistent snack or meal, and to avoid disappointment by an unknown restaurant, choose one of the bistros or brasseries.

THE "BISTROS" AND "BRASSERIES" IN PARIS

There are thousands of restaurants (3,900, including 750 Brasseries and Bistros), and cafés in Paris. The mass of information and publicity offered by Internet, blogs, travel talks, the local or international Press, guidebooks (the red Michelin alone lists 69 bistros and 9 brasseries), Tourist offices, and leaflets in the hotels, makes the choice difficult and hazardous. The following chapter will really skim what in my personal opinion is "la crème de la crème" and a must for the visitor.

THE BISTROS

The word "bistro" comes from the Russian word meaning "quickly." When occupying Paris in 1815, thirsty Cossacks and Russian soldiers would enter any drinking place and shout this word to be served alcohol at once. When they left Paris, the word remained referring to low-class, inexpensive eating and drinking houses. A majority of these places were situated around the Paris Central Market and catered to workers, butchers, fishmongers, etc. At the turn of the century, it became fashionable to frequent these establishments where, apart mingling with the characteristic fauna, one could eat decently at reasonable prices.

Today, bistro or bistrot is the generic word for any drinking place. The Central Market has moved out of Paris.

Only a few original bistros have remained with their 1900 decoration and atmosphere, joined by some modern, quite well decorated replicas.

The Red Michelin guide lists 54 bistros inside Paris.

Here is my selection of the most typical French Bistros where good food and service are provided together with atmosphere. Prices range from 25 to 80€ (wine not included).

PARIS I – Les Halles (ex-central Food Market) and the heart of Paris on the Right Bank.

Tour De Monthlery (Chez Denise)
Rue des Prouvaires, 75001 Tel 01 42 36 21 82 Metro Pont Neuf or Châtelet.

A must, well known by the local jet set... Located behind a rustic half-timbered facade, Chez Denise is one of the last surviving bistros where the wholesale food market workers from Les Halles used to come at all hours to warm up over a typically French meal. Not only is Denise still there behind the zinc bar, the unpretentious bistro doesn't seem to have changed at all. Diners pack side-by-side into the small tables covered with checkered tablecloths, so there's plenty of socializing. The waiters, in their black and white traditional uniforms, are professional, yet their straight-faced teasing is always accompanied by a friendly wink. Old movie posters and paintings decorate the walls; the menu is written on chalkboards that move around the room so everyone can see; and the dishes are simply huge. Be sure to reserve a table, since the dining room fills up quickly!

Chez Clovis
33, rue Berger, 75001 Tel. 01 42 33 97 07

Not far away from Denise's, Chez Clovis is another of the last real bistros left from the old Les Halles food market days. It also managed to keep its pre-World War I atmosphere. Food is superb, especially meats, and served royally for very reasonable prices. The owners and waiters love to tell stories about Paris.

Strangely enough, Chez Denise and Chez Clovis are not very often mentioned by Internet advisers (should we complain?). But the Parisians make no mistake, and without a reservation, it is hard to find a table on any day of the week.

EUROPE DIGEST FOR THE HURRIED TOURIST

Joe Allen
30, rue Pierre Lescot, 75001 Tel. 01 42 36 70 13

If you long for Home American food, this is the place. Just off the former Halles de Paris, decorated as in its premises in New-York or Miami Beach (with red-and-white checkered tablecloths, brick walls, etc.), Joe Allen serves perhaps the best spare ribs in the city. Reservation is a must, as this place is always full. However, prices are expensive.

PARIS II – The Stock Exchange, Banks, Press, and theaters district.

Chez Georges
1, rue du Mail Paris II. Tel. 01 42 60 07 11. Metro: Sentier

Typical original 1900 decor with mirrors, stucco, wall sofas, zinc bar, etc.

If you were to ask Parisian bankers, aristocrats, or antiques dealers from this district near the Stock Exchange to name their favorite bistro for a three-hour weekday lunch, many would choose Georges. The traditional fare, described in authentically indecipherable handwriting, is good, but the atmosphere is better, compensating for the steep prices. In the dining room, a white-clothed stretch of tables lines the mirrored walls, and attentive waiters sweep efficiently up and down. Order one of the wines indicated in colored ink on the menu, and you can drink as much or as little of it as you want (and be charged accordingly).

FRANCE

PARIS IV – City Hall and Pompidou Centre.

Benoit
20, rue Saint-Martin Paris IV. Tel. 01 42 72 25 76.
This is the archetype of the grand bistro.

Just a stone's throw from the Hôtel de Ville (Town Hall), the Pompidou Centre, and the famous Tour Saint-Jacques, Benoit first opened its doors in 1912 and is now one of the last authentic Parisian bistros around. Sold to Group Alain Ducasse in April 2005 by the Petit family, who had been its owners for three generations, Benoit is renowned for its warm and friendly, atmosphere, typical of a family business. In spite of rather high prices (average 60/70€), it is an enjoyable experience.

Rotisserie Du Beaujolais
19, Quai de la Tournelle Paris IV. Tel. 01 43 54 17 47.
Owned by Claude Terrail (La Tour d'Argent).

Situated on the Left Bank, this bistro has a small terrace on the street offering a pleasant view on River Seine's embankments.

PARIS VI – Latin Quarter, just off the Boulevard Saint-Germain (Left Bank).

Procope
13, rue de l'Ancienne Comédie Paris VI. Tel.: 01 40 46 79 00.

The oldest restaurant in Paris, opened in 1686 when

the owner introduced coffee to Paris, this café littéraire near the Faculty of Medicine and the Latin Quarter used to be patronized by Voltaire, Rousseau, Diderot and Benjamin Franklin. It is still a gathering place for writers, actors, journalists, and students (as well as tourists).

PARIS IX (Right Bank)

Au Petit Riche
25, rue Le Pelletier Paris IX. Tel. 01 47 70 68 68 Metro: Richelieu - Drouot

This authentic bistro opened in 1854 near the boulevard Haussmann and its department stores.

Rebuilt in 1880 after the dreadful fire of the theatre "Opera Comique," the restaurant acquired a refined décor that includes warm-hearted multicolored, mosaic paintings and finely engraved window panes.

This is a privileged place for businessmen, journalists, and art collectors frequenting the nearby auction house. In the evening, it serves dinner to clientele from the neighboring theatres.

Chartier
7, rue du Faubourg Montmartre Paris IX. Tel. 01 47 70 86 29. Métro Notre Dame de Lorette / Saint Lazare

350 seats, 16 waiters, 1,500 meals/day. Very reasonable prices. This bistro-brasserie has not much changed over the last 100 years. It is packed and noisy; if you want to get a table immediately, get there by 6pm or risk

a 45-minute wait. The meals are surprisingly hearty, and the house wine is very affordable. The service is friendly but somewhat brusque, so be prepared, but the food is traditional and tasty. It offers perhaps the most affordable prices among the Parisian bistros.

PARIS XV – South West Paris

Troquet
21, rue Bonvin Paris XV. Tel.: 01 45 66 89 00.
Typical troquet (slang shortening of the word bistroquet – small bistro). The owner and chef is Basque and offers some traditional Basque specialties.

PARIS XVII (West end)

Le Relais de Venise (*L'Entrecote*)
271, bd Péreire Paris XVII. (Porte Maillot) Tel. 01 45 74 27 97
This steakhouse serves steak almost exclusively. Be sure to get there early, because they do not take reservations and there will definitely be a wait. You will see people lined up out the door, but the line goes fast, and it is worthwhile! For €25, you can't go wrong.

West Side Kitchen
37 rue Saint Ferdinand Paris XVII. (not far away from Arch of Triumph and Marmottan Museum). Tel. 01 40 68 75 05

EUROPE DIGEST FOR THE HURRIED TOURIST

As an alternative to Joe Allen when tired of French bistros for lunch, this is one of the only eateries in France with an authentic American vibe, which translates into the best sandwiches outside of the U.S.

THE BRASSERIES

In France and French speaking countries, a brasserie is a type of restaurant with a relaxed, upscale setting. The word "brasserie" is French for brewery and, by extension, "the brewing business." In the 19th century, when they began to flourish, brasseries brewed and sold their own beer; they later became distributors for larger breweries. Consumption of beer on the premises led to the offer of food service — a development similar to that of British pubs. After 125 years in circulation, the term "brasserie" has lost much of its original meaning. Today, one can find the word slapped on any sort of joint. The authentic Parisian brasseries, however, are historical and heart-pounding places.

A brasserie offers professional service and printed menus (unlike a bistro, which may have neither). Typically, a brasserie is open every day of the week and serves the same menu all day. The service is always outstanding, and you'll discover that the waiters provide half the fun of a brasserie meal.

In a brasserie, you are not obliged to have a meal. Some tables are reserved for those who want just a drink or a coffee.

The cost of a meal at one of the great brasseries averages €30 to 40 per person with wine, although you can always settle for a simple plate of oysters at about €9. Beware of expensive wine lists, as the best bet is often a *pichet* (carafe) of the reasonably priced and eminently drinkable house wine. You will always eat well at a brasserie, but don't expect Michelin-starred gastronomic standards. Rather than being tempted by the gourmet-sounding dishes, which rarely live up to expectations, stick to classic brasserie fare: a vast plateau of *fruits de mer* (seafood), a steaming plate of *choucroute garnie* (sauerkraut with a choice of meats), *steak tartare* with crispy *frites*, a tasty *andouillette* (chitterlings sausage), or a simple *sole meunière*.

Because finding the genuine article can be tricky, here is a selection of the very best brasseries. No trip to Paris would be complete without a stop at one of them:

Au pied de cochon

6 rue Coquilliere, Paris I. (Tel: 40 13 77 00) Metro: Les Halles

Au Pied de Cochon (The Pig's Trotter) is right by Les Halles.

Open 24 hours a day, it is perfect for a late-night meal. After 2A.M., when not many places are serving good food, the atmosphere really heats up with a colorful mix of stage people, clubbers, and curious tourists.

Bofinger

5-7 rue de la Bastille, Paris I. (Tel: 42 72 87 82) Metro: Bastille

The oldest surviving brasserie in Paris, the perfectly preserved Bofinger is a museum of Belle Epoque decoration. In the centre of the main dining room is a magnificent stained glass coupola, and although the food is excellent, especially the oysters, half the fun of dining here is watching the spectacle going on around you: waiters yelling "Chaud devant!" ("Hot in front!") to clear a path as they balance a gigantic seafood platter; a diva making a grand entrance after a performance at the nearby Bastille opera house; and the occasional clamorous mishap when a server bumps into one of his colleagues, crashing plates and glasses, and diners stop for a moment to applaud the disaster.

Le Train Bleu (above Gare de Lyon Railway Station) Paris XII. Tel. 01 43 43 97 96 Metro: Gare de Lyon

The Train Bleu opened its doors in 1901. Who would expect the Gare de Lyon railway station to host this great table upstairs, facing the railway tracks? This place is a cross between a typically Parisian brasserie and a gourmet restaurant. Andre Malraux granted the Train Bleu restaurant historical monument status in 1972. The Belle Epoque decor is breathtaking, and the food is refined. Coco Chanel, Brigitte Bardot, Jean Cocteau, Salvador Dali, Jean Gabin, Marcel Pagnol, and many others were regulars here.

Still largely unknown, lounges offer superb comfortable leather armchairs, where the traveler can relax while waiting for the departure of his train (without obligation to have lunch).

FRANCE

Brasserie Lipp

151 boulevard St-Germain, Paris VI. (Tel: 45 48 53 91) Metro: St-Germain-des-Prés

With its mirror-lined walls and ceiling, Lipp is the Paris dining spot to see and be seen. Maintaining a tradition of never accepting a reservation, tables are allocated depending on the diner's position in the hierarchy of Parisian social life, with the ultimate humiliation being banished to a table upstairs. Arriving very early, you have a fair chance to be accommodated downstairs if the receptionist likes your look. Regular clients may say that the place has gone downhill since the death of founder and owner Roger Cazes, but that is typical Parisian cynicism. A meal "chez Lipp" is still an unforgettable experience.

Café de Flore

172 blvd, St Germain, Paris VI. Metro : St-Germain-des-Prés.

Just across the Boulevard from Brasserie Lipp, Café de Flore, like its celebrated rival Les Deux Magots, has been a landmark since 1880 and a favorite artist hangout for most of the 20th century. During the German occupation, this was a second home to renowned philosophers Jean-Paul Sartre, Simone de Beauvoir, and Albert Camus, forming the heart of the Existentialist movement.

La Coupole

102 boulevard du Montparnasse, Paris XIV. (Tel: 43 20 14 20) Metro: Vavin

EUROPE DIGEST FOR THE HURRIED TOURIST

Opened on December 20, 1927 with a celebratory cocktail party at which 1,500 bottles of champagne were consumed by the likes of Man Ray, Jean Cocteau, Ernest Hemingway, and Blaise Cendrars, La Coupole has retained its reputation as the essential meeting place for Le Tout Paris, despite a scandalous renovation 10 years ago.

Long gone are the days when Simone de Beauvoir and Jean-Paul Sartre held court here, but with its famous pillars decorated by the artists of Montparnasse, the ghosts of Josephine Baker and Henry Miller, and its famous downstairs ballroom that still swings with salsa and samba bands, La Coupole remains a very special place.

Brasserie Mollard

115 rue Saint-Lazare, Paris VIII. (Tel : 01 43 87 50 22)
Metro: St Lazare

Featuring a 1900 setting that is unique in Paris, the brasserie Mollard is ranked as a historical monument. It was constructed and decorated by E. Niermans, the architect of the Hotel Negresco in Nice, the Hotel de Paris in Monte-Carlo, and the Moulin Rouge.

After more than 100 years of existence, and still well-preserved, it is one of the oldest and most beautiful brasseries in Paris.

Brasserie Wepler

14, Place de Clichy, Paris XVIII. Tel. 01 45 22 53 24
Metro: Place de Clichy

Within walking distance from Pigalle, very authentic

and more than a hundred years old, the Brasserie Wepler is the place to be for the numerous artists around Clichy. After more than 100 years, it has become somewhat of an institution in Paris. Its great specialty is seafood. If you like oysters, this is the place.

SHOPPING IN PARIS

It would take a whole book to have an exhaustive approach to what Paris has to offer the greedy shopper.

Not only is Paris the world's capital for haute couture, perfume, as well as jewelry, it also offers a wide choice of Italian, British and other fashion shops, and innumerable places offering the inevitable junk for tourists.

For high fashion, the main shopping areas are the Rue du Faubourg Saint Honoré, Rue de la Paix, Place Vendôme and around the Church of La Madeleine.

For a wider assortment and more moderate prices, visit the Galeries Lafayette and Printemps. Both department stores are located a few steps away from Opera House.

Galeries Lafayette spreads out over three blocks and seven floors. There is nothing you can't buy here, and there is even a wonderful food hall. If shopping has worn you out, then head to the roof terrace on Level 7, where you get spectacular views of Paris free.

Likewise, at nearby Le Printemps, great views can be enjoyed on Level 9. There are also fashion shows at the Printemps on Tuesdays and Fridays at 10 a.m.

Guidebooks, maps, newspapers, magazines and literature in English can be found at WHS Smith, 248 rue de

EUROPE DIGEST FOR THE HURRIED TOURIST

Rivoli (near the Place de la Concorde).

Brentano's, 37 Avenue de l'Opéra, is a Franco-American bookstore more than 100 years old. It went bankrupt in July 2009 when the renting fees increased 500%. Somehow, an arrangement was made, and the shop reopened in 2010.

Practically all shops and department stores grant a tax refund (see page 4).

African street vendors

These street vendorsare the plague of modern cities. Scores of them haunt such places as the entrance to the Versailles Palace, or the Louvre courtyard, and swarm upon the visitor to sell postcards, watches, sunglasses, fake Gucci bags, souvenirs, and all kinds of junk. As poor and comely as they look, do not indulge in buying anything from them. You would patronize illegal, inhuman activity. These vendors are brought over from Africa by specialized Mafias who confiscate their passports on arrival, give them a load of merchandize for which they are responsible, and put them to work using a well-established strategy. The police try to stop them by arresting them and confiscate their stock, but they are soon out again on the streets. They will then have to work even harder to refund the confiscated stock to the dealer and will have no chance to return to their homeland without money or passports.

FRANCE

REIMS AND THE CATHEDRAL

Population: 180,000 Reims is the capital of the Champagne district. Situated 90 miles from Paris, it is conveniently linked to the Capital by motorway (one-hour drive) or TGV train (45 minutes) and might be an excursion for Champagne lovers.

The city is situated in the vine-growing country where Champagne wine is produced. Wine has been known since antiquity, but Dom Pérignon, a Benedictine monk, created sparkling wine at the end of 17th century by employing a fermentation process. Pommery, Taittinger, Veuve Clicquot - Ponsardin, Piper-Heidsieck, and Mumm have their headquarters in the vicinity, where the wine is stored in large cellars tunneled in the limestone that underlies the district. Most of these cellars are open for tasting. Visits are on a fixed timetable or by special arrangement and are worth the journey.

There are 220 million bottles of Champagne produced there every year, one third of which are exported.

The 13th-century cathedral of Notre-Dame ranks as one of the most beautiful Gothic churches in France. The "Smiling Angel" is famous all around the world. It has a harmonious facade with graceful and expressive statues, fine 13th-century restored stained-glass windows, and a collection of reliquaries. In 498, Clovis, the Frankish king, was baptized at Reims by Bishop Remigius (Rémi); in memory of this occasion, most French kings were consecrated there until 1825 (Charles VII, for example, was crowned there in 1429 in the presence of Joan of Arc).

During World War I, the town was occupied briefly by the Germans in their offensive of September 1914. After evacuating it, they held the surrounding heights, from which they subjected the city to intermittent bombardment over the next four years. The cathedral suffered extreme damage, and the question arose as whether to restore it or raze it to the ground. Fortunately, restoration was decreed and the work continues ever since. In World War II, Reims was again almost completely destroyed, although the cathedral escaped heavy damage. The act of Germany's capitulation in World War II was signed at Reims in May 1945.

FRANCE

PROVENCE - CÔTE D'AZUR

If Paris deserves at least a few days visit (though it would take years to apprehend), Provence and the Côte d'Azur are worth a prolonged stay (many foreigners even retire here). The area offers blue sky 265 days a year and average temperatures never falling below 6° C. The sea, the mountains, the pine trees, the food, the wine, and the *joie de vivre* make this part of France an enjoyable experience. No wonder that Phoenicians, Romans, Queen Victoria, the Rotschilds, German and Austrian nobility, Russian crowned heads, as well as nowadays newly appeared Russian oligarchy, artists and immigrants, golf players from around the world – there are 33 eighteen holes golf courses – peak technology firms, French statesmen, and Renault workers have settled in this part of the world obviously favored by Gods.

Provence belongs to the southeastern region of France known as PACA (Provence-Alpes-Côte d'Azur). For the French, and all northern European countries deprived of sunshine, this is a paradise of sand beaches on the Mediterranean, typical hinterland villages, beautiful sceneries, olive trees, the chant of the cicadas, rosé wine, and exotic food. There is no other place in the world (except perhaps Tuscany) where the sky is so blue, and the air so crystalline. No wonder that a great number of impressionist or modern painters settled there. Practically ignored before WWI, it has become a major point of attraction for summer or even all year long vacationers, due to easier connections by road, train, or plane. Since the end of WWII, the local population has almost doubled, due to the arrival and settlement of expelled North African French residents in the early 1960s, retired people, and services workers and executives from the north of France. Major cities including Marseille, Toulon, Nice, and Aix-en-Provence have tremendously increased their activities and thus their population. This has also brought uncontrolled building development, with greedy promoters erecting ugly lines of concrete buildings wherever possible. Fortunately, the government and local authorities became concerned about this proliferation and now manage to keep it under control, avoiding the concrete disaster of the Costa Brava in Spain. As for the beautiful mansions and villas built on the Côte d'Azur by the rich people in the first half of 20th century, they have almost all become the property of oil magnates, and new Russian millionaires.

Provence - Côte d'Azur is roughly composed of three areas.

To the west of PACA region, Provence proper is the land celebrated by the French poet Mistral and the French author and film producer Marcel Pagnol. It includes the cities of Marseille, Aix-en-Provence, Nimes, Arles, and Avignon. The central region, covering the Department of Var, has two areas: the plains, known as *"Provence verte"* (green Provence), and a mountainous area known as *"Haute-Provence"* (high Provence).

Along the ocean, the mountains of Esterel and Maures offer fantastic views and walks. The largest towns are Toulon, the main base of the French Navy on the Mediterranean,

FRANCE

and Draguignan. The most famous resorts are Saint-Tropez, home of Brigitte Bardot, and Saint-Raphael.

To the east is the Côte d'Azur or French Riviera, which runs from Cannes to the Italian border. It is an uninterrupted succession of towns lining the oceanfront, the most important of which are Cannes, Antibes, Juan-les-Pins, and Nice. Apart from the bigger cities, which have their own history, economy, architecture, and local traditions, Provence is scattered with smaller towns and villages that have curiosities of their own.

Here is a short list of places to visit in Provence:

ARLES

A city of some importance with 55,000 inhabitants, Arles lies on the river Rhône, 32 km from Nimes. It is renowned for its Roman monuments, a Roman arena erected in the 1st century AD, and the ruins of a Roman theatre. The beautiful 11th century Church of Saint Trophime is also worth a visit for its magnificently sculptured gates. Each year at Easter, three days are devoted to bull fighting in the arena, with daily corridas of high standard, and a fiesta in the streets.

Van Gogh spent 15 months in Arles, creating more than 100 drawings and 200 paintings. Henri Gauguin joined him. Arles is also the birthplace of the fashion designer Henri Lacroix, who regularly used the richness of typical Arlesian styles of fabrics.

South of Arles, the National Park of Camargue, a botanical and zoological nature reserve, occupies 328 sq mi in the Rhône delta. It offers a unique approach to more than 400 bird species, as well as raccoons, otters, and beavers. It is also a privileged place for cattle, especially the Camarguese bulls, which are destined for fighting in Arles and Nimes.

The area is also known for its rice production.

AIGUES-MORTES

This fortified town is the extreme western point of Provence. Until the 14th century, Aigues-Mortes was the port where kings and chivalry could embark for the Crusades without having to use a foreign port like Marseille. Saint-Louis sailed from there to Palestine in 1248 along with 1,500 other vessels. The town, built by the same Saint-Louis in the shape of a checkerboard, is completely surrounded by fortified walls. It still looks today as it did in 1300, when the walls were completed.

LES BAUX-DE-PROVENCE

This village, 18 kms north of Arles and 29 south of Avignon, sits right under the ruins of an impressive citadel whose mighty lords refused to submit to the Pope – then residing in Avignon –, the Counts of Provence, and even the King of France.

In 1375, the Viscount Raymond de Turenne had a charming pass-time forcing prisoners to jump over the cliff. Louis XIII had the fortress destroyed, and it was never reconstructed.

It belongs partly to the Grimaldis of Monaco. The

FRANCE

Prince of Monaco has the title of Marquee des Baux. The citadel attracts 2 million visitors each year, all crawling along a single narrow street where scores of shops await the credulous tourist.

SAINT REMY DE PROVENCE

Not far from Les Baux-de-Provence, this charming village and its surroundings became very popular in the 1960s with the French jet-set crowd, who bought or built summerhouses and villas there. It is also the birthplace of Michel de Notredame, known as Nostradamus.

TARASCON

Situated 100 km west of Marseille and 18 north of Arles, the town owes its name to the legend of the Tarasque, a monster who used to emerge from the Rhône River and eat people and animals until it was tamed by Saint Martha. King René's impressive medieval fortress stands sharply on the Rhône's bank. Tarascon is the hometown of "Souleïado", a factory created in 1938 that specializes in printed cloth using patterns made as far back as the 18th century.

NIMES

Population 140,000. Nimes has definitely a passion for bull fighting, as illustrated by the statue of a bull standing on the main avenue.

The first corrida was run in 1863, following Spanish rules. In 1952, Nimes inaugurated the "Feria", a period of festivities lasting five days, during which the entire city is

EUROPE DIGEST FOR THE HURRIED TOURIST

devoted to bullfighting, bull runs through the town, musical bands on the streets, and scores of "bodegas", temporary outlets serving food, "pastis," and Sherry wines.

Ferias take place twice a year, at the end of May and in mid-September. They attract almost one million visitors. It is impossible to find an accommodation in town if not booked well in advance.

Corridas are performed in the Roman arena, which has been converted to accommodate 7,000 viewers. All of the greatest names of bullfighting come to participate. Nimes has welcomed matadors like Luis Miguel Dominguin, Antonio Ordonez, El Cordobes, El Juli, and many others. Nimes is proud of its prestigious Gallo-Roman past.

The Roman amphitheatre is probably the best-preserved arena in the Roman Empire. Twin to the one in Arles, measuring 130 m long, 100 m wide, and 21 m high, it could then accommodate an audience of 24,000 people to enjoy such performances as gladiators' combats.

Another highlight in Nimes is the "Maison-carrée", a small Roman temple built in the 1st century AD. This is the world's best-preserved Roman temple.

Nimes has always been renowned for its textile industry. Arriving in the United States from Europe in the mid-19th century, Oskar Levi Strauss, a Bavarian immigrant, followed the Gold Rush to San Francisco. Hearing of the miners' need for durable pants, he hired a tailor to make garments of tent canvas that he imported to the United States from Nimes via the harbor of Genoa in Italy. The blue canvas "de Nimes" soon became known as "denim," and the harbor "de Gênes" became "d'gene". Thus, the words "denim" and "jean" were born. It is also said that without the canvas from Nimes, America would not have been discovered. Christopher Columbus, preparing for his departure for the Indies, insisted that his three caravels would be equipped with the best quality of sails. The best canvas was made in Nimes and was very expensive. The Queen's treasurer would not accept this expense, which led Columbus to swear that he would give up the exploration trip if not given satisfaction. Finally, the Queen accepted, and Columbus went on to discover America, thanks to Nimes.

When in Nimes, taste the famous *brandade* de Nimes, a marriage of pureed flaked salt cod, olive oil, bread, garlic, and milk. Cod is not found in the Mediterranean Sea; it used to be brought from the waters of Newfoundland. Dried and salted, it could be preserved a certain time and travel uncorrupted.

The recipe demands that the cod be pre-soaked in fresh water for at least 24 hours, changing the water frequently. Grandmothers used to hang it in the water tank of their toilets: the water would eliminate the salt, which would clean the tank at the same time.

PONT DU GARD

Just north of Nimes, and really worth a detour, this Roman bridge is a wonder of the Ancient world. Spanning the river Gardon at a height of 49 m, the three-level arch bridge is part of the aqueduct built by the Romans in the 1st century AD. It was designed to bring 20,000 cubic meters of fresh water daily to the city of Nimes, over a distance of 50 km. The structure is 278 m long and made of blocks weighing between 6 and 8 tons assembled without mortar.

AVIGNON

Right in the center of Provence, 100 km from Marseille, 47 km from Nimes, and 2 ½ hours by TGV from Paris, Avignon is a booming town of 90,000 inhabitants that stretches along the banks of the River Rhone.

A bridge was built between 1177 and 1185 across the river, but it was swept away, damaged several times, and finally never reconstructed. People used to organize dancing parties there, and the bridge was made famous in the song "Sur le pont d'Avignon."

Not much is left from the flourishing Gallo-Roman town, ruined after barbaric invasions in the 5th century. Only in the 11th and 12th centuries did Avignon start to grow under the rule of the House of Anjou.

Its destiny really changed in the early 14th century with the establishment of the Papacy exiled from Rome by the unceasing political troubles and fighting between partisans of Italian States (supported by France amongst others) and partisans of the German Roman Emperor.

From 1309 until 1403, when Benedict XIII fled Avignon, a succession of eight Popes brought liberty and prosperity to Avignon. Population jumped from 5,000 to 40,000, and magnificent mansions and palaces were erected, drawing masses of architects, builders, painters, and sculptors from all over Europe.

FRANCE

The Palace of the Popes, built over a period of 40 years, was the largest princely residence of its time. Both a fortress and a palace, it covers an area of 15,000 m2 (2.6 acres).

Avignon is also known for its Festival d'Art Dramatique (Festival of Theatre, Dance, and Music) founded in 1947 by actor/director Jean Vilar. For two weeks in July, two festivals, one official and the other unofficial, organize scores of theater, music, and dance performances in every possible place and in the streets.

MARSEILLE

Marseille is the Capital of the PACA region (Provence–Alpes – Côte d'Azur). It forms the third largest metropolitan area after Paris and Lyon, with a population of 1,700,000. Economic conditions and political unrest in Europe brought successive waves of immigrants in the 20th century. Greeks and Italians started arriving at the end of the 19th and in the first half of the 20th century. Almost 40% of the city's population was Italian at that time. Russians came after the 1917 Revolution, Armenians in 1915 and 1923, and the Spanish after 1936. From the 1950s onward, the city has served as an entrance port for over a million immigrants to France, mainly from sub-Saharan Africa and North Africa, among which an influx in 1962 of 150,000 French settlers fled from Algeria. Today, more than 70,000 city residents are of Maghrebian origin, mostly from Algeria. The second largest ethnic group is from Comoros in the Indian Ocean (45,000 people). These immigrants give the city a mixed appearance and have created a large Franco-African quarter.

EUROPE DIGEST FOR THE HURRIED TOURIST

History

Marseille, the oldest city in France, was founded in 600 BC by Greeks from Phocea under the name of Massilia. Facing a threat from an alliance between Etruscans, Carthaginians, and Celts, the Greek colony asked for protection by the expanding Roman Republic and thus was brought into the complex Roman market, to which they exported goods and wine. This arrangement lasted until the rise of Julius Caesar, when Massalia joined the losing side in the civil war, led by Pompey, and lost its independence in 49 BC. During the Roman era, Massilia adapted well to Roman status and habits. It was during this time that Christianity first appeared. According to Provencal tradition, Mary Magdalene evangelized Marseille with her brother Lazarus. She is believed to have retired in a grotto in the mountain now called la Sainte-Baume ("the holy grotto") and was buried in the Basilica of Saint-Maximin-la-Sainte-Baume, 60 km east of Marseille. With the decline of Rome, the town fell in the hands of the Visigoths, later succeeded by the Franks. Emperor Charlemagne granted civic power to Marseille, which remained a major trading port and gained much of its wealth and power under the administration of the Counts of Provence in the 10th century. The bubonic plague decimated the city in 1348 and intermittently until 1361. As a harbor, Marseille was the first place in France to encounter the epidemic, and more than half of the population died during that period. In 1437, the Count of Provence René of Anjou, who succeeded his father Louis II of Anjou as King of Sicily and Duke

FRANCE

of Anjou established himself in Marseille and fortified the harbor. He granted privileges to the town, which became a flourishing city. Marseille was united with Provence in 1481 and then incorporated into the French Kingdom after King René's death. The local population enthusiastically embraced the French Revolution and sent 500 volunteers to Paris in 1792 to defend the revolutionary government. On their march into Paris, they sung a rallying call to revolution composed in Strasburg by a young Army officer named Rouget de l'Isle. This song, "La Marseillaise," became the French national anthem. During WWII, the Germans occupied Marseille from November 1942 to August 1944. A large part of the old town was destroyed in an attempt to reduce opportunities for resistance members to hide and operate in the densely populated old buildings, and because the quarter was a refuge for all kinds of trafficking. The destroyed quarter was rebuilt in the 1950s without any architectural taste and planning, probably due to lack of funding. The current rebuilding of the docklands and the restoration of 19th century's Haussmanian buildings were fortunately better planned.

WHAT TO SEE AND TO DO IN MARSEILLE

Marseille is a big, bustling city with an atmosphere but without many exciting places to visit.

Le Panier. Situated behind the reconstructed buildings along the quays of the old harbor, this quarter reflects the old Marseille look with its narrow streets and derelict buildings.

EUROPE DIGEST FOR THE HURRIED TOURIST

The Notre-Dame-De-La-Garde Basilica. Built in 1835 and towering above the city, the basilica is topped with a gilded statue of the Virgin Mary called La Bonne Mère ("the merciful mother"). The terraces of the Basilica offer a fascinating panorama on the city and the sea. The Basilica is accessible by car or by bus n° 60 from the Old Harbour.

The Old Harbor. This is the preferred strolling place of the Marseillais. Both sides are lined with shops and restaurants; a lively fish market opens every morning at the bottom of the harbor.

AN APPROACH TO MEDITERRANEAN FOOD AND DRINK

Local food and drinks owe their origins to the various countries boarding the Mediterranean Sea, and reflect the local southern production: olives, tomatoes, eggplant, citrus fruit, etc. Aromatic herbs, thyme, basil, rosemary, lemon thyme, tarragon, laurel, and sage are widely used in Provencal cuisine. Fish plays an important part in many recipes. Wine has been consumed since the Antiquity, and rosé wine has become a favorite drink, especially in the summer. Pastis is a must before meals.

Bouillabaisse (bwee-yah-BEHZ) is perhaps the most celebrated Provencal dishes. This is a complete meal based on three fishes, *rascasse* (scorpion fish), *grondin* rouge (red gurnet), and *congre* (conger eel). Other kinds of fish and shellfish are usually added to the dish, which cooks gently in olive oil. The name comes from *bouille* ("boil"), and *abaisse* ("lower"), meaning that one should lower the fire when it comes to boiling. It is seasoned with onion, tomato, saffron, garlic, thyme, bay leaves, sage, fennel, and orange peels (the seasoning is just as important as the fish). A glass of white wine or brandy gives the meal its final touch. The broth and fish are served with thick slices of bread buttered with *rouille*, a kind of mayonnaise with garlic, saffron, chili, fish liver (or fish bouquet), and crushed boiled potato.

Aioli: mayonnaise made with olive oil and strongly flavored with crushed garlic. It is usually offered with fish, boiled potatoes, carrots, and turnips.

Pissaladière: a cross between a pizza and a pie with onions, tomatoes, garlic, and aromatic herbs.

Daube: beef or boar, macerated in wine, onion, carrots, garlic, herbs and spices for 24 hours and then stewed for at least 3½ hours.

Tapenade: a Provencal appetizer consisting of pureed or finely chopped olives, capers, and olive oil. This paste is generally spread on slices of bread.

Anchoïade: a paste made of finely chopped black olives, garlic, and anchovy paste spread on toasted slices of bread; it may also be used as stuffing for fillets of beef.

EUROPE DIGEST FOR THE HURRIED TOURIST

Aniseed-based drinks and Pastis

Aniseed-based drinks have been distilled for centuries around the Mediterranean: Ouzo in Greece, Raki in Turquey, and Arack in Lebanon. All are part of the country's social life and are usually accompanied by *meze*, a large offering of various appetizers. In Italy, Sambuca is drunk *con la mosca*, with two or three coffee beans that are crushed and eaten to complement the flavor of the spirit. Aniseed was brought to Sicily 1,000 years ago by the Arabs, who drank it steeped in water (zammu). It started to be distilled in the Middle Ages. In Spain, there are two types of Aniseed: secco (dry) and dolce (sweet). The town of Chichon, near Madrid, has been renowned for anis since the 18th century.

Pastis is the main social drink in the south of France. Many brands are produced, mostly in Marseille or its surrounding region. The most famous are Ricard and Pernod. Pernod was originally produced as absinthe. A doctor called Pierre Ordinaire, who used it as medicine, developed absinthe in 18th century. He called his elixir after one of the ingredients he used: wormwood (artemisia absinthum). Widely drunk throughout the 19th century, absinthe was banned when its hallucinogenous properties were discovered. It is still produced in the Czech Republic.

FRANCE

SHOPPING

- **Typical Provencal cloth**. Printed with bright colors, amongst which lemon yellow, olive green, cobalt blue, and vermilion, it figures Mediterranean motives, such as fruits, olives, or flowers, and is used for ladies skirts, table-clothes, napkins, and other garments.
- **"Santons"** (clay figures, displayed traditionally in Christmas cribs).
- **Nougat** from Montélimar, confectionaries made with sugar and/or honey, roasted nuts (almonds, walnuts, pistachios, hazelnuts), and sometimes chopped candied fruits.
- The famous **Savon de Marseille** (soap on basis of olive oil), praised for its purity and washing qualities.

EUROPE DIGEST FOR THE HURRIED TOURIST
CANNES, NICE, AND THE FRENCH RIVIERA

CANNES

Cannes is situated in a large bay overlooked by the red Esterel Mountain and the first slopes of the Alps. Cannes owes its prosperity to Lord Brougham, who was forced in 1834 by the threat of cholera to halt in the fishing village as he was journeying to Nice. He found the place so beautiful that he built a villa there and praised the site among his compatriots.

Today a big, busy city bustling with tourism and luxury commerce, Cannes spreads along the seafront, boarded by the Boulevard de la Croisette, a magnificent avenue with palm trees, sandy beaches, luxury shops, and five-stars hotels such as Carlton, Majestic, and Martinez.

Cannes is world-renowned for its Film Festival, which takes place every year in May.

NICE

Nice is perfectly situated between the sea and the mountains. It is the fifth largest town in France with a population of 450,000 and still growing. Its airport is the second biggest in France for traffic. Its pleasant climate has made it the leading resort city of the French Riviera. Along with Cannes and Antibes, Nice is now a part of a huge agglomeration which extends over 30 km along the Mediterranean Sea. The name of Nice comes from Nikaïa, the Greek word meaning "victory." Signs of the people who lived there

FRANCE

400,000 years ago can be found in many places. In the 4th century B.C., Greeks from Marseille established here a successful center for trading.

In the 1st century B.C., during the invasion of Gaul, the Romans built a large town on the hill now called Cimiez, complete with thermal baths, an arena, a theatre, even a system for central air heating. As a result, Nice became one of the most modern and pleasant cities in the antique world. After the fall of the Roman Empire and various barbaric invasions, the Counts of Provence took over; however, in 1388, the inhabitants rose against them and refused domination. The country passed to the House of Savoia (Italians), and the Count of Savoia triumphantly entered the city. The town and surroundings became Italian and received the name of County of "Nice." Except for a few interruptions, it remained the property of Savoia until 1860, when King Victor Emmanuel II offered it to France as thanks for the intervention of Napoleon III in the Italian independence war against the Austrians. A referendum was organized, and the people agreed to the unification.

In 1763, an Englishman named Smollett, author of travel books, crossed the Var River on the back of a local peasant. When he wrote about the enchantment of Nice, England learned about the almond trees blossoming in the middle of January. The English were quickly convinced that Nice was the place for spending winter, and hundreds of them began visiting the region. By 1820, there were already more than 100 English families residing there. Even Queen Victoria spent the last seven winters before her death in

EUROPE DIGEST FOR THE HURRIED TOURIST

Nice. She used to walk along the avenues of Cimiez, surrounded by her Hindu servants and her Scottish Guard – imagine the bewilderment of the locals when they saw the way the British dress... In 1868, Nice and the French Riviera were linked to Paris by rail and therefore to London. The following year, the Prince of Monaco announced that all taxes would be abolished in the nearby principality (the income from the casino and the hotels covered the entire principality budget). That provoked a rush to the region by international jet setters, nobility and big fortunes, princes and grand-dukes of Russia, kings, and lords from German countries, etc. In 1890, 22,000 people spent the winter in Nice; in 1910, 150,000. There were increased investments in hotels, residences, and city development. Artists were welcomed, and painters, such as Matisse and Chagall, as well as musicians came to live there. This boom lasted until the 1950s when the English colonial pensions were cancelled, and French workers were allowed paid vacations. The English colony dissolved, and the British Consulate closed its doors in 1975. That was the end of a century of glory and happy life, a time when the most fashionable definition of happiness was to be born in Cannes, live in Monte-Carlo, and die in Menton. During those golden years, a number of builders, workers, and servants were needed, and thousands of Italians came to settle there, which is why there are so many Italian names around. Today, the Italians visiting the Côte d'Azur are not workers but rich tourists, and the working force is African, living in large, low-rate, concrete blocks looking like suburbs from Algiers or Tunis.

Foreign residents now buy or build houses in the mountains above Nice or further out in Provence (Saint-Tropez, Saint Rémy de Provence, or the Luberon mountain) and tax evaders go to Monte-Carlo, where, as a result, a square meter of flat can cost up to $15,000.

Important people linked with Nice

Andre Massena: one of Napoleon's greatest generals born in Nice 1758.

Giuseppe Garibaldi: born in Nice July 1807(see here under).

Niccolo Paganini: born in Genova in 1702, died in Nice 1840. Considered one of the greatest violinists of all times, he was also a merry fellow and a gambler. When he lost his violin in a card game, a wealthy merchant lent him a Guarneri and refused its return. Paganini kept this violin until his death. He lived at 23 Rue de la Préfecture and used to scandalize his neighbors by imitating cats' meows with his violin.

Isadora Duncan: born in San Francisco in 1877, she was the pioneer of modern dancing. She resided in Nice in September 1927, when she was strangled by her scarf when it was caught in the wheel of her convertible car.

William "Billy" Mitchell : U.S. Army officer born in Nice in 1897, he promoted the idea of a strong independent air force and became the Commander of the U.S. Air Force in WWI. Despite conservative resistance, his ideas were finally accepted and put into effect during WWII.

Pierre Auguste Renoir settled in Cagnes in 1905 and

stayed there for the last 14 years of his life.

Marc Chagall died in Saint Paul de Vence in 1985 (see hereunder).

Henri Matisse died in Nice 1954 (idem).

WHAT TO SEE AND DO IN NICE

The **old town**, with its narrow Italian-looking streets, its small cafés, restaurants, and shops.Cours Saleya, a lively square in the old town, with its colorful flower and fruit market, and the open terrace cafés and restaurants

Place Massena

Built around 1850, this magnificent square is the heart of Nice, at the eastern part of the Promenade des Anglais. Around it are shopping streets bustling with activity.

Nearby, from Albert 1er Gardens/ Quai des Etats-Unis, a mini-train takes you around the major sights of Nice. This is a very nice way to see the town without having to walk.

Promenade des Anglais

During the development of Nice, the English preferred to stay outside the town and built houses along the sea. In 1822, a clergyman by the name of Lewis Way collected money from his countrymen to pave the path running along the seashore, which became known as the Promenade des Anglais. Today, this 2.5 mile-long line of buildings overlooks the sea and the eight-lane boulevard. Running from Place Massena parallel to the Promenade, a small, lively pedestrian street offers a large selection of restaurants, cafés, and shops.

Hotel Negresco, on the Promenade des Anglais

Henri Negresco was the son of an innkeeper in Bucharest. He left at the age of 15 for Paris and then the French Riviera, where he became very successful. As the director of the Municipal Casino in Nice, he chose a beautiful place to build a sumptuous hotel, which was completed in 1912. Unfortunately, his hotel was requisitioned by the Army in 1914 to serve as a hospital, and Henri Negresco died before he could profit from his investment. A visit to the lobby and the lounges is a pleasant experience, together with a tea or a drink at the bar.

Russian Orthodox Cathedral: An extraordinary building.

Tsarevitch Nicolas Alexandrovitch, son of Alexander II, died of sickness in Nice in 1864. Forty years later, his fiancée Maria, who married Alexandre III, Nicholas' brother, decided to build a chapel on the spot where the Tsarevitch died. The Cathedral was later erected on the site with funds provided by the Tsar Nicholas II, using the same plan as the St. Basil Cathedral in Moscow. It is the largest Russian Orthodox cathedral outside of Russia.

Marc Chagall and Henri Matisse museums
Marc Chagall

Marc Chagall was born on July 7, 1887 in Russia and died March 28, 1985 in Saint Paul de Vence, where he is buried. He created a genre virtually of his own with his lively, large-scale renderings of Russian village life and his illustrations of folk tales and Bible stories. Chagall's highly imaginative and very personal style took shape after he moved to Paris in 1910, where he became associated with the celebrated school of Paris. His dreamlike images had some of the characteristics later associated with surrealism, for example, in "I and My Village" (1911; Museum of Modern Art, New York).Chagall returned to Russia in 1914 and welcomed the Russian Revolution of 1917. He became Commissar of Fine Arts in 1918 in his native Vitebsk and director in 1919 of the local art academy and later in Moscow, where he designed sets for the Kamerny State Jewish Theater.

His return to Paris in 1923 inaugurated the second half of his career. The "Bride and Groom of the Eiffel Tower" (1939) is representative of this period, along with his illustrations for "La Fontaine's Fables" (1952) and for the Bible (1957). Both projects were commissioned by the renowned Parisian art dealer Ambroise Vollard. At the suggestion of New York's Museum of Modern Art, Chagall spent World War II in the United States, where he designed for the ballet, including Stravinsky's "Firebird" (1945). The popular success of his designs for the dome of the Paris Opera in 1964 led to a commission for two enormous murals in the foyer of New York's Metropolitan Opera House. At the age of 90, Chagall became the first living artist to be exhibited at the Louvre. The Marc Chagall Museum in Nice houses the most important permanent collection of the painter's works, most of which were donated to France by the artist.

FRANCE

Henri Matisse

Born on December 31, 1869, Matisse, one of the most important French painters of the 20th century, became the leader of the Fauvist Movement in 1900. He started spending winters on the French Riviera after WWI, most of the time in Nice, with periods of travelling to Normandy and abroad. In the 1940s, he had a villa built in the village of Vence, on the hills above Nice. He offered to paint the Chapelle du Rosaire belonging to the local Dominican nuns, who had taken care of him during a severe disease in 1941. This chapel, completed in 1951, is open to the public. After 1950, he lived in a large studio in the Old Hotel Regina, overlooking Nice, while he was suffering from asthma and heart trouble. Henri Matisse died in Nice on November 3, 1954. His Museum, located in the Villa des Arènes, a splendid patrician villa in Cimiez, houses a large collection of Matisse's works and personal effects.

Museum of Modern and contemporary Art (Mamac)

Mamac is the popular name given by the Niçois to the Museum of Contemporary and Modern Art. On the third floor, a large exhibition of pop art includes works by Warhol, Wesselman, Lichtenstein, Oldenburg, and Rosenquist.

Le Chateau

This fortress and stronghold was built in the 12th century on the hill above the town, on the remainders of the first Greek settlement in Nice. First the property of the Counts of Provence, the fortress passed to the Duchy of Savoia in 1388. In 1706, when the Duke Victor-Amedee II went into conflict with Louis XIV, the king of France had the stronghold dismantled after a siege of 54 days, and bombardment by 114 artillery guns.

In 1876, Sir Thomas Coventry, an eccentric lord, installed a cannon on a terrace in the castle ruins; it was fired every day at noon (a Scottish tradition). By 1879, all clocks in town were set after this canon fire.

The University

The University of Nice is located in the Valrose Palace. It was built in 1865 as a winter residence on 25 acres of land by Von Derwies, the builder of the Transsiberian, a billionaire, and a friend of the Tsar. Von Derwies had an isba transported from Russia and rebuilt in the garden, where it is still to be seen.

Garibaldi Square

Built in the 19th century by the Duke of Savoia as the starting point of the road to Turin, the square was renamed several times until it received the final name of Garibaldi in 1870.

Giuseppe Garibaldi

Giuseppe Garibaldi, born in Nice on July 4, 1807, was Italy's most brilliant soldier of Risorgimento and one of the greatest guerrilla fighters of all time. While serving in the navy of the Kingdom of Sardinia-Piedmont (1833-1834),

FRANCE

he came under the influence of Giuseppe Mazzini, the prophet of Italian nationalism. He took part in an aborted republican uprising in Piedmont in 1834.

Facing a death sentence, he managed to escape to South America, where he lived from 1836 to 1848. There, he took part in struggles in Brazil and helped Uruguay in its war against Argentina, commanding its small navy and, later, an Italian legion at Montevideo. The handsome warrior achieved international fame through the support of the elder Alexandre Dumas.

Wearing his colorful gaucho costume, Garibaldi returned to Italy in April 1848 to fight in its war of independence. His exploits against the Austrians in Milan and against the French forces supporting Rome and the Papal States made him a national hero. In May 1860, Garibaldi set out on the greatest venture of his life, the conquest of Sicily and Naples. Sailing from near Genoa with 1,000 Redshirts, Garibaldi reached Marsala, Sicily, and proclaimed himself dictator in the name of Victor Emmanuel. At the Battle of Calatafimi (May 30) his guerrilla force defeated the regular army of the king of Naples. After plebiscites, he handed Sicily and Naples over to Victor Emmanuel when the two met on October 26. Angered at not being appointed Viceroy in Naples, Garibaldi retired to his home on Caprera, off Sardinia. Subsequently, during the Franco-Prussian War (1870-71), Garibaldi led a group of volunteers in support of the new French republic. Without Garibaldi's support, the unification of Italy could not have taken place when it did. A gifted leader and man of the people, he knew far better than Cavour or Mazzini how to stir the masses, and he repeatedly hastened the pace of events. He died at Caprera on June 2, 1882.

WHAT TO EAT IN NICE

Add the following local specialties to the list of Mediterranean food:

Salade Niçoise This salad plate consists invariably of tuna fish, lettuce, tomatoes, French beans, hard-boiled eggs, boiled potatoes, and anchovies.

Pan-Bagnat Literally translated as "bathed bread," this large, round shaped bun is soaked with olive oil and garnished with tuna fish, tomatoes, onions, salad, hard-boiled eggs, salted anchovies and black olives.

Ratatouille niçoise Diced eggplants, zucchini, tomatoes, and onions are fried separately in olive oil, mixed with black olives and Provencal herbs, and then simmered for 20 minutes before serving.

Socca This is a thin pancake made with chickpea flour and olive oil.

OTHER HIGHLIGHTS

Pétanque

Originating in 1907 in the region of Marseille, this bowling game (from the *pes tancats*, fixed feet), involves players who have their feet anchored in a small circle throw hollow metal balls as close as possible to a small wooden ball called a *cochonnet* (jack). The Pétanque is played by 17 million people in France, mainly during summer vacations.

FRANCE

Carnaval de Nice
This festival takes place during the two weeks before Mardi Gras. Huge parades of flower-covered floats move along the Promenade des Anglais, and brilliant nighttime displays are organized.

SAINT-PAUL DE VENCE

Saint-Paul de Vence, a 30-minute drive from Nice, is a well-preserved fortified village of the Middle Ages. Its present celebrity started when artists such as Modigliani, Soutine, Bonnard, and Signac began to stay at the local modest inn, La Colombe D'or, whose owner accepted their paintings in payment. This was also the case for Matisse and Vlaminck. Today, La Colombe d'Or is a museum with paintings by MIRO, BRAQUE and MATISSE. The food, served in the restaurant and on the terrace decorated by Fernand Léger, is excellent. As in Eze, the center of the village has become, a tourist attraction, with scores of art galleries and shops. Some real art objects can be found at preposterous prices, but most of the merchandise is the usual tourist stuff and junk. Still, the atmosphere of these narrow streets with their succession of merchants is worth a visit, except in the middle of the summer, when the crowds make it difficult to get around. Nearby is the famous Maeght Foundation, a museum devoted by Aimé and Marguerite Maeght to modern art. Housed in modern concrete and brick buildings, spreading on the gently sloping hill, and enlightened by numerous terraces shaded by pine trees, the museum offers a permanent exhibition of sculptures and paintings by Giacometti, Calder, Miro, and others as well as temporary exhibitions of contemporary artists.

FROM NICE TO MENTON

In addition to the highway, which runs on the top of the mountain above the sea, three more scenic coast roads (*corniches*), at different levels, link Nice with Monaco, Menton and the Italian border. The Basse Corniche (Low Coast-Road) winds along the sea coast, crossing small villages, the Moyenne Corniche (Middle Coast Road) goes through Eze-Village, and the Grande Corniche (Great Coast Road) runs on the top of the mountain through La Turbie and Eze Pass. All are pretty drives offering spectacular views over the Coastline.

VILLEFRANCHE AND CAP-FERRAT

After 1945, this beautiful gulf harbored an American naval base until France left NATO. It is a well-preserved site, and real estate is very expensive.

EZE

This picturesque, isolated village is located on a rock spike 427 m above the sea. The steep narrow streets are lined with carefully restored houses, which are now boutiques and artist studios. In past centuries, inhabitants used

FRANCE

to go down the hill to fish and climb back the 1,410 feet. Happily, this was made on mules' back, when one was rich enough to have one. Today, hordes of tourists, brought by buses, crowd the streets to look at the picturesque sceneries and enjoy the splendid views of the Riviera (one can even see Corsica on a clear day).

MONACO AND MONTE CARLO

A steep rock overhanging a well protected creek, this is why the Phoenicians from Massalia (Marseille) chose this site to establish their colony more than twenty-six centuries back. Melkart called Mono-Ikos ("single god") was the god of the local Ligurian inhabitants, and gave its name to the settlement. In the times that followed, Monaco suffered repeted change of hands between Romans, Franks, and Lombards. In 1191, Holy Roman Emperor Henry VI granted suzerainty over the area to the city of Genoa, the native home of the Ligurians. A fortress was built on the rock and, to create a strategic stronghold, Genoese set about creating a settlement around the base of the Rock to support the garrison; in an attempt to lure residents from Genoa and the surrounding cities, they offered land grants and tax exemption to new settlers.

In 1297, Francis Grimaldi, a Guelph Genovese, seized Monaco by disguising his commando as Franciscan monks. Under the sovereignty of the Republic of Genoa, the Grimaldis acquired Menton in 1346, and Roquebrune in 1355, enlarging their possessions.

After a period of French control from 1793 to 1814,

EUROPE DIGEST FOR THE HURRIED TOURIST

the principality was re-established in 1814, only to be designated a protectorate of the Kingdom of Sardinia by the Congress of Vienna in 1815. Monaco remained in this position until 1860, when Sardinia ceded to France the surrounding county of Nice (as well as Savoy).

During this time, there was unrest in the towns of Menton and Roquebrune, which declared independence. This unrest continued until the ruling prince gave up his claim to the two towns, and they were handed over to France in return for four million francs. This transfer and Monaco's sovereignty was recognized by the Franco-Monegasque Treaty of 1861. Deprived of 95% of his property, and left without much income, the Prince granted concession for a gambling house, which was to become the Casino of Monte Carlo. In 1872, the casino received 160,000 visitors. In 1933, France and Italy authorized the opening of gambling houses, which ended Monaco's monopoly, cutting its contribution to the state budget from 95% to 4%. By that time, many private citizens and companies had already settled in Monaco (where there are no taxes), and the fortune of Monaco continued to grow nonetheless. The current ruler, Prince Albert II, succeeded his father Prince Rainier III in 2005.

Monaco has a population of 30,000 inhabitants, only 5,000 of whom are real Monegasques who vote, pay no income tax, and have no military duty. However, 210,000 residents work in private companies, and 15,000 workers commute every day from France and Italy. Millions of tourists visit Monaco every year, and hotels are always full.

FRANCE

Although the currency is the Euro, Monaco has its own stamps and a separate telephone network.

Monaco hosts the annual Formula One Monaco Grand Prix, an automobile race that runs through the town. Prices for renting a flat or a single balcony with a view on the streets where the cars race range from $15 to $20,000/week for 25 to 30 people; a suite with a terrace and a nice view of the race from the Hotel de Paris costs up to $25,000 for a 4-night minimum stay.

Monaco Oceanographic Museum.

The museum has a splendid view of the sea and contains hundreds of beautiful species of fish in its aquariums. It was built 100 years ago by the founder of modern Monaco, Prince Albert I. The Museum has long been associated with Jacques Cousteau, who fascinated generations of TV viewers with his amazing undersea adventures.

Visit of the town

The Principality has two centers of interest:

The older part, the Monaco rock, occupied by the Palace, old administrative buildings, the Cathedral, and the Oceanographic Museum;

Facing the "Rock" (*le rocher*) on the other bank of the Monaco harbor, Monte-Carlo offers to tourists, gamblers and wealthy magnates from the whole world its luxury hotels, residential areas, and probably the world's best-known Casino.

EUROPE DIGEST FOR THE HURRIED TOURIST

Access to the Monaco rock is prohibited to cars not registered in Monaco or the near-by French Alpes-Maritimes department. However, underground car parks are conveniently situated, with large lifts to the Palace square. There are also seven public escalators and elevators (all free) that help negotiate the steep slopes of the city.

Due to its configuration, walking around Monaco and Monte-Carlo may be rather tiring. The best solution to see most of the Principality is to take a ride on the "Azur Express", a fun tourist train that leaves in front of the Oceanographic Museum, and makes in 30 minutes a tour all over Monaco and Monte-Carlo. The trip costs €7.

The **Monaco A.T.P. World Tour tennis** tournament takes place in April, and the 2.5 million € prize attracts the greatest tennis champions.

Changing of the guard

It occurs daily at 11:55 A.M. in front of the Prince's Palace.

Ventimiglia

A few miles from Monaco, crossing the border to Italy, Ventimiglia is the first resort on the *Riviera dei fiori*, the Italian equivalent to French Riviera. On Fridays, a huge and lively market attracts thousands of visitors and buyers to Vengtimiglia,

GERMANY

GERMANY

OFFICIALLY NAMED THE Federal Republic of Germany (Bundesrepublik Deutschland), the country is bordered to the north by the North Sea, Denmark, and the Baltic Sea; to the east by Poland and the Czech Republic; to the south by Austria and Switzerland; and to the west by France, Luxembourg, Belgium, and the Netherlands. The territory of Germany covers 137, 847 sq mi.

The name Deutschland, the land of Deutsch, comes from the name of the first Evangelist of Germania Theodiscus.

With 81.8 million inhabitants as of January 2010, Germany has the largest population among member states of the European Union and is home to the third-largest number of international migrants worldwide.

THE GOVERNMENT

The Bundeskanzler (Federal Chancellor) heads the Bundesregierung (Federal Government) and thus the executive branch of the federal government. He or she is elected and is responsible to the Bundestag, Germany's parliament. Germany, like the United Kingdom, can thus be classified as a parliamentary system.

By contrast, the duties of the Bundespräsident (Federal President) are largely representative and ceremonial. The President is elected every five years on May 23 by the Federal Assembly (Bundesversammlung), a special body convened only for this purpose, comprising the entire Bundestag and an equal number of state delegates, selected especially for this purpose. Federal legislative power is divided between the Bundestag and the Bundesrat (Federal council). The Bundestag is directly elected by all German citizens, while the Bundesrat represents the regional states (Länder).

The Reichstag building is the seat of the Bundestag. The Bundestag consists of 598 or more members, elected to a four-year term. Germany was reunited after the fall of the Berlin Wall on November 9, 1989. This reunification brought the population to 81 million inhabitants. The former Federal Republic of Germany (West Germany) was already the first economic power in Europe (except for the U.S.S.R. at that time). The very poor state of East Germany's economy, its derelict industry and crumbling buildings, brought a very heavy burden onto West Germany's economy. However, knowing the German potential resources, and its capacity to work hard, there was no doubt that United Germany would, in a matter of years, rank as the number one power in Europe.

GERMANY

HISTORY

Once upon a time, in the thick forests covering the earth, the Germans to be were very quiet: they didn't know they were Germans, and were mingling with their indo-European cousins in the center of the Euro-Asian continent. Around 1500 BC, the Hellenics migrated south to Greece, Italiots towards the Italian peninsula, and the Celts spread all the way from Turkey to Portugal. They halted in the southern part of Germany, leaving the northern part to their cousins from Scandinavia. Around 150 B.C., pushed southwards by the cold climate of Denmark, Teutons, Saxons, Sueves, Goths, Cimbrians, and other numerous tribes began to invade the Gauls (present-day France). They were driven back in 105 B.C. by the Roman General Marius but tried again 40 years later, and Julius Caesar pushed all these hordes back again.

The Romans called them Germani, meaning "all of the same blood" in Latin. They lived in the open, had no towns, and traded amber and furs in exchange for jewels. Their gods were all terrible, crippled or mutilated. When they died, they believed they went up to the Walhalla of gods. Today's Germans still have remnants of this pathos and desperation. The Emperor Augustus decided to put an end to these incursions and to conquer Germany. He dispatched his general Varus and three legions with 30,000 soldiers. Arminius-Hermann, a German who had served as an officer in the Roman army, raised an army of several tribes and trapped the three legions in a vast and thick forest. Of

EUROPE DIGEST FOR THE HURRIED TOURIST

the three legions, no one survived; only skulls, nailed to the trees, were later found. Hermann became the first German hero. In a state of shock, the Romans withdrew, and established the "Limes", a line of fortified towns from the Rhine to the Danube. Now the Germans knew about the delicious ways of living in the south. Attacks continued for the next 300 years. When the Roman Empire weakened, all of these populations, pushed southwards by the Hun invasion, fought their way through and invaded Italy in 375. Ethnical groups separated: Visigoths pushed further south to Spain whilst Angles and Saxons crossed the sea to invade England. Following the capture of Rome, there was a period of incessant migrations, coming mainly from the east and the north. When the Huns showed up in Italy, the Germans allied with the Romans to push Attila back. Then came the time of final settlement: in Germany, the Thuringen created the future Thuringia, Sueboz the Schwaben, Marcomans Bavaria, Franks the Franconia (from which they later immigrated to Gaul), Alamans the south part of Germany and Switzerland, Saxons the Saxonia, etc. One people were to federate all these populations, the Franks: after conquering Gaul and naming their leader Clovis as Emperor, they submitted the major part of the German land in 511. Nations were founded: the North became Saxony; the South, Austrasia (origin of the name "Austria"). Meanwhile, the Vikings made bloody incursions along the coasts; the Anglo-Saxons established a kingdom in England; and the Franks created a west kingdom in France and an east kingdom in the region now called Franken (Franconia).

GERMANY

The feudal system developed in the middle Ages and brought some stability to European nations, after the Barbaric era that had followed the fall of the Roman Empire. It was led by strong characters at every level of the hierarchy. At the highest level were the kings and emperors, who were crowned by the Pope. Below them were dukes and counts, the most powerful aristocrats in Germany. Equal in rank were the bishops. Since any king could hardly maintain a regular army, they were dependent on their barons and dukes. They often found it very difficult to keep them under control; some were powerful reigning princes, who ruled their land as an independent state and maintained costly courts. In 751, the Carolingian dynasty took over from the Merovingians, the dynasty originated by Clovis the Frank. The summit was achieved by Charles the Great, who ruled the major part of Europe.

Called to rescue by the Pope Leon III, Charles saved him from his personal enemies, and restored him on the papal seat. In gratitude, the Pope crowned Charles the first Roman Holy Emperor. After Charles' death, his only son inherited the Empire but could not manage to keep it united, as his own four sons started fighting against each other. This marked the end of united Europe, which dislocated into a great number of dukedoms. When the last of the Carolingians disappeared without an heir, the rulers of the Four Nations, Suabia, Franconia, Bavaria and Saxony, assembled to elect the King of Germany. The crown was given to a Frank, but then later passed to a Saxon dynasty – the Ottos. Otto "the Great" submitted his opponents, crushed an invasion by Hungarian hordes, and recreated Charles' empire, However, France had grown as a separate power, and was not involved. Without France, Otto's empire became the Holy Roman Germanic Empire, a purely German entity. Under the control of great archbishops, Germany stabilized. The German Emperor was the most powerful sovereign in the West, elected by the assembly of "Great Electors",the three main Archbishops, the King of Bohemia, the count palatine of the Rhine, the Margrave of Brandenburg, and the Duke of Saxony. The Emperor was considered equal in power to the Pope, who confirmed the title. However, the Pope was not a Great Elector, and competition for supremacy soon arose between the Emperor, supported in Europe by the Ghibellins, and the Pope supported by the Guelfs (see page 253). At this time, Germany was bordered to the north by Scandinavia and the Vikings, dangerous neighbors who had recently destroyed the town of Hamburg, and to the west by the growing power of France. Expansion was only possible to the South, towards Northern and Central Italy, where the Emperor came into conflict with the Pope's armies.

From the 10th century until the fall of Napoleon and the Vienna Congress in 1815, the German land was a patchwork of states, some of them powerful, like Bavaria, Saxony, and Prussia, all of them fluctuating in their alliances with Austria, England, France, and Spain. At that time, history was not only made on the battlefields but also with great skill and intrigue behind the walls of castles and palaces. In that respect, the acquisition of land through

GERMANY

marriage was a very significant factor. The Catholic Church was deeply involved. During the Vienna Congress, following Napoleon's abdication, a German Confederation of 39 autonomous states, including Austria, was proclaimed. Between 1815 and 1871, a strong nationalist feeling appeared; Prussia and Austria competed for their supremacy over the confederation, leading to a state of war. Finally, Bismarck, the head of the government of Prussia, eliminated Austria at Sadowa in 1866, defeated France in 1870, and proclaimed the German Empire. After the fall of the third Reich, the country was divided into four military zones: American, Russian, British, and French. The zone under Russian control became more and more aggressive, resulting in the split in 1949 that created West and East Germany. This split lasted 50 years.

Today, Germany is divided into 15 Länder (states) and the city of Berlin.

The main towns are:

Berlin (pop. 3.3 million), the capital of Germany since June 1991 ;

Hamburg, home to over 1.8 million people, is the second-largest city in Germany and the eighth largest in the European Union. The port of Hamburg is the third-largest port in Europe after Antwerp and Rotterdam, and the eighth largest in the world.

Many American people and places claim to have "invented" the Hamburger steak. One widely accepted version states that the Hamburger steak originated on the German Hamburg-America line boats, which brought emigrants to America in the 1850s. There was at that time a famous Hamburg beef, salted and sometimes slightly smoked for keeping on a long sea voyage. As it was hard, it was minced and sometimes stretched with soaked breadcrumbs and chopped onion. It was popular with the Jewish emigrants, who continued to make Hamburg steaks, with fresh meat when they settled in the U.S.

Munich (pop. 1.2 million), capital of Bavaria (and the seat of the Bayern football club), famous for beer and BMW;

Cologne, the oldest and the fourth largest town in Germany with more than a million inhabitants, is located on both sides of the Rhine River. It is a major cultural centre of the Rhineland.

The University of Cologne is one of Europe's oldest universities.

The city's famous Cathedral, started in 1248, is the seat of the Catholic Archbishop of Cologne. Although heavily damaged, the Cathedral survived miraculously the extensive bombing during WWII.

The first settlement on the grounds of what today is the center of Cologne was founded in 38 BC by the Ubii, a Germanic tribe. In 50 AD, the Romans founded Colonia on the Rhine and the city became the provincial capital of Germania Inferior in 85 AD.

During World War II, Cologne endured 262 air raids by the Western Allies, which caused approximately 20,000 civilian casualties and almost completely wiped out the center of the city. During the night of 31 May 1942, Cologne was the site of "Operation Millennium", the first

GERMANY

1,000-bomber raid by the Royal Air Force in World War II.

With its seven Rhine bridges and ten motorways, Cologne is an important hub for the north-south transit. Each day more than 1,000 trains enter or leave Cologne Hauptbahnhof (main station).

Cologne is the birthplace of Eau de Cologne, the famous alcohol fragrance crated by John Maria Farina, whose 245th death anniversary is commemorated in 2011. Today, original Eau de Cologne is always produced in Cologne by both the Farina family, and by Mäurer and Wirtz who bought the 4711 brand in December 2006.

Essen and **Dortmund**, in the Ruhr area, most important coal and steel centers, home of the Krupp family;

Frankfurt (pop. 627,000), the commercial capital of Germany, a center for scientific research, and birthplace of the Frankfurter sausage;

Nuremberg (pop. 500,000), is almost 1,000 years old. Heavily destroyed during WWII, it is today an active center in economy, administration, and trade.

Leipzig and **Iena**, home of Leica cameras;

Heidelberg, a city of students with its magnificent castle.

Stuttgart, has a population of 650,000. Capital of the Baden-Württemberg state, it lies in the center of a densely populated area. During the Cold War, Stuttgart became home to the joint command centre of all United States military forces in Europe, Africa and the Atlantic (US European Command, EUCOM). The Stuttgart area is known for its high-tech industry. Some of its most prominent companies include Daimler AG, Mercedes-Benz, Porsche, Bosch, Hewlett-Packard and IBM.

The German culture has immensely influenced the world, mainly in religion, music, and literature. The greatest contributor to the world of knowledge and communication in which we live today was Johannes Gutenberg, the inventor of modern printing, born around 1400 in the restless city of Mainz.

The 15th century was a period where people were coming out of the medieval blackout, striving for new ways of thinking, and looking towards new horizons. Universities were established, knowledge was gathered, and the earth was explored. Gutenberg's invention came at the right moment, when people were eager to learn, and by the beginning of the 16th century, there were already 300 printers established in 60 German cities.

One of the first beneficiaries of this new way of communication was Martin Luther who made good use of it to promote his ideas.

Famous German musicians
John Sebastian Bach (1685 – 1750)
Dietrich Buxtehude (1637 – 1707)
Johan Pachelbel (1653 – 1706)
Georg Friedrich Haendel (1685 – 1759)
Georg Philip Telemann (1681 – 1767)
Ludwig von Beethoven (1770 – 1827)
Carl Maria von Weber (1786 – 1826)
Robert Schumann (1810 – 1856)

GERMANY

Johannes Brahms (1833 – 1897)
Richard Wagner (1813 –1883)
Karlheinz Stockhausen (born 1928)

Germany has also produced stars of rock and punk music, including Nina Hagen and The Scorpions.

Famous German philosophers
Gottfried Leibnitz (1646 – 1716)
Emmanuel Kant (1724 – 1804)
George William Hegel (1770 – 1831)
Friedrich Nietzsche (1844 – 1900)
Arthur Schopenhauer (1898 – 1860)
Martin Heidegger (1889 – 1976)
Herbert Marcuse (1898 – 1989)

Writers
Berthold Brecht (1898 – 1956)
John Wolfgang von Goethe (1749 – 1832)
Thomas Mann (1875 – 1955)
Erich Maria Remarque (1898 – 1970)
Gunther Grass (born 1927)

Snow White and The Seven Dwarfs is a German fairy tale, written by Jacob and William Grimm at the beginning of the 19th century.

Artists
Lucas Cranach (1472 –1553)
Albrecht Durer (1471 – 1538)

EUROPE DIGEST FOR THE HURRIED TOURIST

Scientists
Wilhelm Roentgen (1845 – 1923)
Max Planck (1858 – 1947)
Albert Einstein (1879 – 1955)

Another major German contribution of all times is Martin Luther (1483 – 1546), the founder of the Lutheran Reformist Church.

Today, German famous figures appear mainly in sports and cinema: In sports, Franz Beckenbauer has played 103 times in the German national soccer football team and is considered as one of the greatest European players ever. Famous tennis players include Steffi Graf, and Boris Becker (nick-named "boom-boom" for his heavy service). Michael Schumacher has been many years the winner of the car World Formula 1 racing cup.

Famous names in cinema include:
Friedrich Murnau
G.W. Pabst
Fritz Lang
Ernst Lubitsch
Reiner Werner Fassbinder
Wim Wenders
Marlene Dietrich

GERMANY

THE GERMANS

Their language sounds like something awful, and they are considered as square-jawed robots. However, their cars outperform all others, their soccer teams seldom lose, and it has taken two world wars and millions of dead to quench their thirst of power. Behind this facade lies a nation uncertain about where it is, how it got there, and where it goes. They are fearful of what other nations think of them: Are we becoming arrogant? Is our tolerance failing? Are we slipping back to the old days? On one hand, they retreat into the angst of the soul, psychoanalysis, and high culture. German music and movies are full of fairies, dragons, and mythical or tormented characters (probably a consequence of their pagan ancestral barbaric origin). Poets like Goethe and composers like Wagner have emphasized this. On the other hand, they seek refuge in order and system (i.e. the State laws and the Bundesbank, State Bank). A common phrase is "Alles in Ordnung", meaning that everything is in order, as it should be. The streets are clean, the houses painted and decorated, the litter is in the bins. They appreciate quality and are happy to pay for it. They are well dressed, well shod, drive solid cars, and live in double-glazed and centrally heated homes equipped with lots of reliable gadgets. Germans pride themselves on their efficiency, organization, discipline, cleanliness, and punctuality. Germans consider themselves as ordinary people. They love *gemütlichkeit* (coziness): give them a *wurst* (sausage), a beer, and another German to talk about politics or the stress of life, and they will be content. German manners are somewhat square. Don't expect an apology if somebody bumps into you on the sidewalk. You might get a stern look, and even perhaps a muttered remark about getting in the way and your mental well-being. You might be shocked by German bluntness and directness. The Germans are unable to admit being wrong or having made a mistake. However, they are always polite, and will address you as Sie. It would be unforgivably rude to do otherwise. They will shake hands on any occasion: meeting, parting, arriving, leaving, or on agreeing something. The handshake must be firm: beware your finger bones.

GERMANY

FRANKFURT-AM-MAIN

Frankfurt am Main is located on the Main River about 32 km (20 mi) east of its confluence with the Rhine. Its name comes from Frankonovurt ("the fort of the Franks").

The city has an area of 222 sq km (86 sq mi) and a predominantly Protestant population of 628,000.

Mentioned as early as 793 AD, Frankfurt is one of Germany's oldest cities. Recent archaeological findings indicate that a Roman post occupied the site as early as the 1st century. Charlemagne held his imperial assembly in Frankfurt in 794. In 843, it became the capital of the East Frankish kingdom. The Golden Bull of 1356 designated Frankfurt as the seat for the election of the Holy Roman emperors. In 1815, the city became the capital of the German Confederation. In 1866, Frankfurt was occupied by the Prussian army and incorporated into Prussia, thus losing its cherished free-city status. In 1871, the peace treaty ending the Franco-Prussian War was signed there; it came to be known as the Treaty of Frankfurt.

Situated at a convenient crossroad between south and north Germany, Frankfurt developed into Germany's most important commercial, industrial, and transportation center. It is a major railroad junction as well as an important river port. Its airport is the second largest in Europe (after London's Heathrow), with some 5,000 flights per week.

It is home to manufacturers of chemicals, pharmaceuticals, leather goods, and electrical equipment; the city is also noted for banking (the Germans call it "Bankfurt").

EUROPE DIGEST FOR THE HURRIED TOURIST

One of the first stock exchanges was created there at the end of the 16th century, and the Rothschild dynasty developed its banking tradition in the 18th century.

Frankfurt is the seat of the European Central Bank. 196 foreign banks have an office in Frankfurt, as well as 336 credit agencies, 9,000 lawyers, and 59 Chambers of Commerce. The trade fairs are among the most important in the world.

There are also 47,000 students, 33 theatres, 37 museums, 110 art galleries, and 38 discotheques.

Behind the wealth, however, hides Frankfurt the poor, with its flocks of immigrants from East Germany and other Eastern European states, as well as Turkish laborers.

GERMANY

HEIDELBERG

Heidelberg stretches between the Neckar River and forested hills, giving it an enchanting Look. This is the town of the romantics and the seat of the oldest and best-known university in Germany, founded in 1386, the third in Europe after Prague and Vienna.

For more than six centuries, students lived in the old town, gathering in the old taverns to drink beer and discuss the world. Today, the University has 29,000 students, of which 15 % come from abroad. 437 professors, 3,400 non-professional teachers, 500 guest professors, or lecturers teach in the 15 different faculties. In 1907, the lower jawbone of a man was found in a wall near Heidelberg. This bone was dated back to 500,000 years BC, the earliest presence of humankind in Europe. The man to whom it belonged received the name of Homo Heidelbergensis. The Romans had a permanent camp here, with a wooden bridge across the Neckar River, until 260 AD. The first permanent settlement dates back to the 5th century and is mentioned in documents dated 769, under the name of "Bergheim." The village belonged to the Archbishops of Worms and was taken over by the house of Hohenstaufen in 1155. The name "Heidelberch" is mentioned in a document in 1196.

Conrad von Hohenstaufen became Pfalzgraf of the Rhine (Count Palatinate – pfalz derives from the Latin word palace). In 1195, the Palatinate absorbed the House of Welfen (later nicknamed "Guelfs") by marriage. In 1342, the Palatinate became a vassal state of Bavaria, under the ruling of the Wittelsbach family.. The Palatinate was granted its autonomy from Bavaria in 1329 and was then ruled alternatively by the two branches of the Hohenstaufen family, who received the title of Princes Electors of the Palatinate. This autonomy was confirmed by the "Golden Bull" of 1356. During the Middle Ages, Heidelberg was the political center of the Rhine Palatinate land (Rhein-Pfalz). For the next 200 years, the successive Electors of the Palatinate, or Grand Officers of the Holy Roman Empire embellished Heidelberg.

In 1618, political and religious dispute developed in Prag, part of the Holy Germanic Empire, between the current ruling catholic Habsburgs and Protestant noblemen. A number of these penetrated the Royal Palace and threw two royal governors out of a window. They then called the Palatinate prince elector Frederic V, who was a Protestant, to be crowned King of Bohemia in the place of Habsburg. This incident sparkled a Catholic-Protestant war that was to last 30 years, engulf all the European nations in the struggle, and extend as far as Caribbean Islands, the South Atlantic, and the Indian Ocean. It was a war without mercy, but mainly the common people suffered from it. Historians claim that in some states of Germany civilian population losses were 50% or more. Heidelberg was taken by the Habsburg troops; the famous Palatinate Library was seized, and sent to the Vatican as a gift to the Pope. After the Peace of Westphalia, the Palatinate, and the title of Great Elector went to Bavaria. Later, Karl-Ludwig, the son of Frederic V, managed to restore well-being in the Palatinate. Anxious to preserve peace in the region, he married his daughter Liselotte to the Duke of Orleans, brother of Louis XIV. Soon after, Liselotte's brother, heir to the throne, died without succession. Louis XIV seized the opportunity and claimed the heritage due to his sister-in-law. His demand was rejected, so he invaded the Palatinate. In 1689, French troops took Heidelberg and destroyed it completely before setting fire to what remained. The two enormous dungeons of the castle were blown-up . It took more than 100 years for the city to be rebuilt, most of it in Baroque style. A new university opened in 1803.

At the end of WWII, Heidelberg citizens succeeded in handing the town unscathed to the American Army. Heidelberg was then chosen as the headquarters for the U.S.A.F.E.

The beautiful architecture and the enchanting surroundings of Heidelberg have attracted many writers and painters. Romanticism gave the students heroic ideas. Heidelberg is the city where young student-officers used to duel with swords. Even during the Second World War, German officers proudly exhibited scars from wounds received at dueling when at the university.

The town has many catering places, but a worthwhile visit will be the *Studentenlokalle*, where students used to meet:

Schnookeloch: Haspelgasse 8

Roter Ochsen: Hauptstraße 217

EUROPE DIGEST FOR THE HURRIED TOURIST

THE CASTLE OF HEIDELBERG

The Heidelberg Castle ranks with the Acropolis in Athens and the Palace of Versailles as one of the sights most worth seeing anywhere in Europe. It receives 3 million visitors each year. In 1303, a document mentions two castles, one on the top of the hill, which was destroyed by lightning in 1537, and the other one at the present location. Prince Elector Ruprecht III began the construction in 1400, when he became King of Germany under the name of Ruprecht I. The castle was embellished by his various successors until its destruction by the Habsburg Armies in 1622. Ruprecht III had a rather simple building built on the left side of the Tower Gate doorway, which is today the main entrance.

On the Tower Gate, the keystone above the entrance, a masterful and legendary piece of Gothic sculpture, represents two twin-like angels holding a wreath of flowers surrounding a pair of compasses. As the legend goes, the charming twin boys came almost every day to visit their father, the master builder. Shortly before completion of the work, they fell from a scaffold and were killed. The father flowered their tombs every day with white roses and was unable to finish building. One night, he dreamed of his two sons appearing before him as angels; the next morning, he found next to his bed the same fresh and fragrant roses as he had put on his sons' graves the day before — but the white roses had become red. The master-craftsman went back to his work and created the magnificent keystone depicting his boys, the wreath of roses, and the compasses as

GERMANY

his signature. Prince Elector Ludwig V(1508 – 1544), the main architect of the castle, prolonged Ruprecht's building with a Library, destroyed by French troops in 1688, and the King's Hall, containing also the women's quarter. From 1508 to 1544, Ludwig V fully renovated the defensive walls and built the gatehouse, service quarters, and lodgings for the guard on the right side of the entrance (where the ticket office is).

From 1556 to 1559, Prince Elector Otto Heinrich built the Renaissance palace seen on the right side. On the lower floor of this building, the Apothecaries' Museum, the most extensive exhibition of its kind in the world, presents a unique collection of instruments, pharmaceuticals, laboratory equipment, and books dealing with pharmacy and medicine from the 16th to the 19th century. In front, closing the square, the Friedrichsbau, a palace built by Friedrich IV (1583 – 1610) displays over-sized statues of emperors, kings, and princes of the Wittelsbach dynasty. The statues are good replicas, made during the renovation works of 1897 to 1900; the originals are now inside the building.

Life in the castle was joyful and eating and drinking were topics. Wine was the main beverage, of which some 175,000 gallons were permanently stored in the cellars. Daily consumption was up to 500 gallons, and this is why Prince Elector Johann Casimir had the palace vaulted cellar equipped with a barrel to contain the wine for the whole population of the castle: a barrel containing 31,000 gallons. It was later changed for a barrel containing 49,000 gallons. Finally, in 1751 it was replaced again by the present vat, made out of 130 oak trees and containing 58,000 gallons. It is the largest wine barrel in the world (26 feet long by 21 high). On the wall, facing the vat is a statue of the dwarf Perkeo. He came from South Tyrol (Italian side) and was the Court jester and Keeper of the Vat in the beginning of the 18th century. His name is supposed to have come from his habitual reply in Italian to the question whether he would have another glass of wine: Perche no? (Why not?"). Tradition says that he died from having accepted to drink a glass of water. He is the symbol of the Heidelberg Carnival, and said to be the inventor of the clock nearby.

GERMANY

MUNICH

With more than 1.3million residents, Munich, the capital of Bavaria, is the symbol of German economic success. You will see an incredible number of yuppies, called *schicki-micki*, rushing around in Mercedes or Porsche convertibles, or the latest BMW model. There are also many longhaired, hippie-looking youngsters, riding bicycles.

Located a few kilometers from the Alps, it is one of Germany's most attractive cities.

Founded in the 9th century near a Benedictine monastery and named "Muniche", meaning "monk" in old German, the town belonged originally to the Duke Henry the Lion. In 1180, it passed into the hands of the Wittelsbach family. In 1328, Louis the Bavarian of the Wittelsbach line was proclaimed king of Germany, then Emperor. The town developed rapidly, due to its situation as a crossroads between north and south, east and west Europe. Found of knowledge and culture, the Wittelsbach made Munich an arts and architectural center. The line of the kings of Bavaria came to an end when Luwig III abdicated in the November 1918 revolution, which brought onto the scene Hitler's new German Workers' Party.

Munich is the home of Adidas, Siemens AG (electronics), MAN (truck manufacturing), and BMW, among other big companies, along with the largest German breweries and banks.

Munich is a leading location for science and research with a long list of Nobel Prize laureates from Wilhelm

EUROPE DIGEST FOR THE HURRIED TOURIST

Conrad Röntgen in 1901 to Theodor Hänsch in 2005. The University is one of the largest in Germany, with 44,000 students, of which 15% are foreigners. Some 700 professors and 3,600 academic staff members conduct research and teach in the university's 18 faculties.

Munich has its own Latin quarter, Schwabing, where famous residents have lived, amongst which Richard Wagner, Thomas Mann, author, Wassily Kandinsky, painter, Joseph Ratzinger, now Pope Benedict, former Archbishop of Munich-Freising , Wilhelm Röntgen, Nobel Prize winning physicist, Max Planck, Nobel Prize winning physicist, Rainer Werner Fassbinder, film director, Vladimir Lenin, Adolf Hitler, and others.

Richard Strauss was born in Munich, Einstein studied at the university, and the refrigerator was invented there. Today, Schwabing has become a centre of fashion shops and pseudo artists. The amount of tourists has a bit altered the real student atmosphere, but it is still a place with scores of restaurants, and the much-frequented *kneipen*, a cross between a café and a tavern, where much of the Munich social life takes place. You can spend hours there, drinking and eating at any time of the day; some organize concerts in the evenings or other cultural events. Türkenstrasse is the nicest place to visit.

Munich is paradise for beer-lovers. According to the Munich Statistical Office, the city has seven major breweries that produce annually 550 million liters (more than 145 million gallons) of beer.

Ein Bier, bitte ("One beer, please") is an essential phrase

GERMANY

for tourists visiting Bavaria.

The *kellers* (cellars), *biergarten* (beer gardens) and *bräuhausens* (breweries) welcome millions of thirsty beer drinkers each year (wines are available too). The premises are enormous halls or gardens with long wooden tables with benches on both sides, accommodating hundreds of people, with a Bavarian brass band playing the oompah-pah, thousands of people rocking arm-in-arm at the sound of the music.

If the place is crowded, just find a place where no one is sitting, greet your fellow beer drinkers, and check that the seat is free. When the weather is good, everyone sits outside drinking an incredible number of one or two liter beer mugs and downing innumerable *wurst* (a generic word for a wide variety of meat sausages) and *bretzels* (pretzels). The other food is usually excellent and may include grilled pork ribs or roasted knuckles, roasted goose, goulash beef stew, sauerkraut, grilled fish, and other specialties at bargain prices.

Here are four of the "must-visit" beer establishments:

Hofbräuhaus

Perhaps the best known and most aesthetically pleasing of Munich's beer halls. Hofbräuhaus is located in the heart of the city's pedestrian zone. One of Munich's most attractive and recognizable landmarks, Hofbräuhaus celebrated its 420th birthday in 2009. It can accommodate 5,000 people.

EUROPE DIGEST FOR THE HURRIED TOURIST

Augustinerkeller

Another huge beer-hall seating 5,000, the Augustinerkeller is not far from Hofbräuhaus. Originally an Augustiner monastery, it first began brewing beer in 1328. The beer served here is, of course, Augustiner. Traditional Bavarian *weisswurst* with potato salad is at its best, while more daring guests can taste the jellied ox mouth.

Biergarten am Chinesischer Turm

In the heart of the Englischer Garten (English Garden) stands the famous 'Chinese Tower'. Built more than 200 years ago when the Chinese artistic influence was highly popular, it is now surrounded by one of Munich's most popular beer gardens with a seating capacity of 7,000.

Königlischer Hirschgarten

This Europe's largest beer garden (8,400 seats) also features a charming deer park. Traditional Augustiner beer is served here.

If looking for a quieter place serving not only Bavarian but also continental food, the three following restaurants will prove a good choice:

Zum Dürrnbräu

Im Tal 21, Phone: (089) 22 21 95

For those courageous enough to confront the essentials of traditional Bavarian fare, it is a famed destination. Here you can enjoy all kind of organs, such as intestines, lungs or heart, plus goodies like pig's feet or head, and the like. They also serve dishes that are more conventional.

Fisch Witte
Viktualienmarkt 9, Phone: (089) 22 26 40

This place is a real gem. Unfortunately, the whole world thinks alike, and whether you fancy fish soup in the morning or half a dozen oysters in the afternoon, the place will be crammed, so make a reservation. Once you squeeze your way in, however, you'll enjoy wonderful food, service, and friendly fellow diners.

Schelling Salon
At the corner of Schellinggasse and Barrerstrasse, in Schwabing. This smaller place, run by the same family for 125 years, features inexpensive, simple food, and plenty of atmosphere.

By the way, did you know that Munich claims to have invented the *wurst*? The earliest Bavarian document relating to *wurst* dates back to 1595. However, the town of Arnstadt, in Thuringia, recently discovered a receipt from 1400 that includes intestine for a fried sausage. Still, the Munich locals maintain that they have evidence of sausage back around 1300. Will there be a Sausage War in Germany?

A short encyclopedia of *wurst*

Germany is the world's leader in the production and

variety of meat sausages. Here is a non-exhaustive list:

Frankfurter Wurst: the nearest equivalent to the hot dog
Bratwurst: veal, pork or beef, finely chopped meat (brat meaning "minced")
Knackwurst: short, plump sausage smoked over oak wood
Bockwurst: veal or pork sausage, usually eaten with bock beer
Rindswurst: made of pure beef, and praised by kosher diners
Currywurst: pork sausage highly seasoned with curry and ketchup. It is the most popular today in Germany (Germans eat yearly 800 million of them).
Jagdwurst: minced meat ("hunting sausage")
Weisswurst: a Bavarian specialty made of veal and fresh pork bacon, highly seasoned with parsley, onions, lemon, and herbs (*weiss* means "white")

Munich is a happy town. During the year, at least 13 events and festivals give the Munich people the opportunity for amusement (and beer drinking). Among them, the *Fasching* (Carnival) from the end of January through Fat Tuesday is a must. All local professional or student associations, sport clubs, institutions, schools and universities organize every day, balls, and parties. A wonderful way to gather and meet new friends (boys or girls, bachelors or married)… The March beer festival, *Maibock*, celebrates the arrival of new beer. This coincides with the May Tree

GERMANY

Feast, when a big pole with the Bavarian emblems is erected on the main square in all villages on the 1st of May. From the end of November through Christmas Eve, the *Christkindlmarkt* (Christmas market) is held in Marienplatz.

The acme of it all is of course the famous Oktober Fest celebrated from September 15 through the first Sunday in October. More than 6 million liters of beer, 90 spit-roasted steer, 450,000 roasted chickens, and 250,000 pairs of sausages are downed by 7 million visitors crammed in the 14 enormous festival canvas halls erected on the Wiesn (Oktoberfest grounds), which offer tables and seating for 100,000 patrons. The 16-day annual festival offers some 200 sideshows, carnival rides, and other amusements, so you'll find always something to do.

Munich is also a place for culture, featuring theaters, museums, publishers, movie studios, and fashion designers – the yearly fashion show attracts buyers from the whole world.

PLACES TO SEE IN MUNICH

This cosmopolitan metropolis has a rather small downtown center, which is easy to cross on foot. The rest of the town looks like a village, with small houses and trees everywhere. It has one of the largest parks in the world: the English Garden, which is bigger than Central Park in New York.

Marienplatz

This astounding square is the hearth of the city, taking

its name from the Mariensäule, a column topped with a golden statue of the Virgin Mary, patron of the town. The column was erected in 1632 to commemorate the end of Swedish occupation during the Thirty Years War.

The impressive New Town Hall, on the north side of the square, was built at the end of XIXth century in a neo-gothic style, and hosts the city government. It has a great tower with a curious touristic attraction: the Glockenspiel, a kind of carillon with moving figures and music that plays everyday at11 a.m. and 12. To the east side stands the old city hall (Altes Rathaus), built in 1470. This building was completely destroyed during WW II, and reconstructed after old plans and pictures.

To the left of the New TownHall, appear the twin characteristic onion-bulb towers of the Frauenkirche (Cathedral of Our Lady), probably the best known symbol of Munich. Built in the 15th century in late Gothic style, it is the largest church in Bavaria.

Marienplatz, now a pedestrian zone, attracts yearly millions of tourists, and a large crowd forms every day to watch the Glockenspiel performance.

Viktualienmarkt

Established in 1807 by decree issued by Maximilian I, Viktualienmarkt (literally, victuals market) was built to replace a much smaller market that had once served the needs of the growing city of Munich.

With more than 140 shops and stalls, It is a lively place, and a favorite with gourmets.

GERMANY

Viktualienmarkt is often the site of festivals and other special affairs, offering traditional and folkloric events, music and dance, and much more.

Residenz

The Palace of the Wittelsbach, it was originally a stronghold built in the 14th century. Successive local rulers added or transformed the building, making it a conglomerate of various styles. It was almost destroyed during WWII, and its restoration took 40 years.

Olympia Park

It was built for the 1972 Olympic Games on a large hill erected after 1945 with the remains from the ruins from bombardments during WWII. The stadium can accommodate 72,000 people; the nautical complex, 14,000. The TV tower is 1,000 feet high and features a revolving restaurant. The Olympic village is used today for student lodging.

Deutsches Museum

Located on the Isar River Island, this is one of the biggest museums in the world, with 300 halls. It covers 14 acres. This is also the most important museum in Europe for science and technology.

ZAM (Zentrum für aussergewoehnliche Museen)

Literally "Center of out-of-ordinary museums." This place features museums of paddle cars, corkscrews, chamber pots, Easter Rabbits, etc. One department is devoted to

EUROPE DIGEST FOR THE HURRIED TOURIST

the Empress Elisabeth of Austria-Hungary, spouse of Franz Josef I, most commonly called "Sissi", played by Romy Schneider in her film trilogy.

BMW Museum is located near Olympia Park in Munich and was established in 1972. It deals with the history of the car manufacturer.

GERMANY

NEUSCHWANSTEIN AND LOUIS II

"Mad king Ludwig", as he has been sometimes called, Louis II Wittelsbach of Bavaria, was born in 1845 in Nymphenburg, a royal palace located near Munich. Visconti magnificently staged his life and death in a film called "Ludwig." He preferred art and music to government and war. Megalomaniac and eccentric, he ruined his kingdom building the extravagant Neuschwanstein castle, and palaces taking Louis XIV's Versailles for model. In 1886, his ministers, weary of his immoderate spending, orgies, and other follies, accused him of insanity, and had him deposed. Disappearing from his apartments, he was found 36 hours later, drowned in the nearby lake. together with his personal doctor. Nobody knows what really happened. Louis spent most of his childhood in the palace of Hohenschwangau (The Highland of the Swan), which was built by his father, Maximilian II. This gave him ideas for his own architectural projects. The construction of Neuschwanstein ("The New Swan Rock"), began in 1868, after Louis spent months trekking in the mountains to find a suitable location. Looking like a precursor of Disneyland fairy castles, it took 465 tons of marble, 1,500 tons of stone, 400,000 bricks, and 20 years of work. It was not finished when Louis II died. In the same time, Louis had another palace built: Linderhof, which was inspired by Louis XIV's Versailles. In 1878, he commissioned the building of a third royal palace on an island of Lake Chiemsee, which was also to be a replica of Versailles. The building was never completed.

EUROPE DIGEST FOR THE HURRIED TOURIST

BERCHSTESGADEN

Berchtesgaden is surrounded on three sides by Austrian territory. The opening of its salt mines in the 12th century was the beginning of many centuries of bitter rivalry with Salzburg. The ancient salt mines are still in operation. Austrian troops occupied the town in 1704, and it was annexed to Austria in 1805. Following a brief period of French rule, it passed over to the Bavarian kingdom in 1810.

It was a major resort and recreational centre during the Allied occupation after WWII.

On the Obersalzberg, 1,500 feet above the town, were the chalets of Adolf Hitler, Hermann Göring, Martin Bormann, and other Nazi leaders, all equipped with air raid shelters, barracks, and various installations. Hitler often stayed at his chalet, called Berghof; this is where he compelled Austrian Chancellor Kurt von Schuschnigg to accept the German domination of Austria in 1938. This is also where Hitler met the British prime minister, Neville Chamberlain, for their first face-to-face discussion of his demands on Czechoslovakia. For the purpose of propaganda, the Nazi Party had 60,000 postcards printed showing a photo of Hitler on the Obersalzberg with a small, pretty, blond girl. Shortly after it was discovered that the girl was Jewish and the Party wanted to destroy the postcards, but Hitler liked the picture so much that he ordered it to be distributed nevertheless. Destroyed in an Allied air attack in April 1945, the Berghof's ruins were leveled in 1952, and trees were planted on the site. An elevator cut in solid rock connects with Hitler's private retreat on top of the Eagle's

Nest mountain, which is now a teahouse.

KÖNIGSSEE

A few miles south of Berchtesgaden, this is perhaps the most picturesque lake in Bavaria and one of the loveliest sceneries in Europe. It is highly recommended to take the nearly 2 hours return boat trip to the south of the lake, which departures every 30 minutes.

Salzbergwerk Berchtesgaden
The salt mine mentioned above, which contributed to the wealth of Salzburg and Bavaria, is open to the public, and visits are organized. The tour takes about 1½ hours. Tel. from Germany: 08652/6002 (from Austria: 0608652/6002).

OBERAMMERGAU: HISTORY OF THE PASSION PLAY

The tradition of the Passion Play dates back to the 12th century. It was originally a mystery play performed as a part of church services to dramatize the suffering and death of Christ. Over the ages, the play took many forms throughout Europe, with the life of Christ as a focal point. The rise of the Protestant Reformation and its questioning of Roman church doctrine hastened the demise of all of the play's performances. All, that is, except for the Passion Play of Oberammergau. In 1633, the Black Plague was sweeping over Europe, killing large numbers of people. Carried by the armies fighting in the Thirty Years War (1618–1648), the flea-borne disease found its way into the remotest mountain villages. In a desperate attempt to isolate themselves, the people of Oberammergau blocked the entrances to their village. In October 1632, one homesick villager who had been a laborer in a nearby farm could not stand to be away from his family for the Church Dedication Feast. He slipped past the guards and rejoined his family. Unfortunately, he brought the dreaded infection with him. Within three days, he was dead, and Oberammergau was in the grips of the disease. By the summer of 1633, nearly 100 people had died.

The villagers pleaded with God for relief, pledging to perform a re-enactment of the Passion of Jesus if God would save the town. The deaths stopped; since that day, the villagers step on stage once every 10 years to fulfill their promise. The first play was performed in 1634 in the choir loft of the church. It quickly outgrew the church and moved to the churchyard and then to a nearby field, where a modern theater was built in 1930. The village people plan, produce, and act in the production. Only natives or those who have lived in the town for 20 years are eligible to audition for parts. The costumes and sets reflect the centuries-old tradition in their design and authenticity. Cast members grow their hair and beards to match their biblical roles, as no wigs or makeup are allowed. Real animals share the stage with the cast.

The Passion Play, performed during the summer of 2010, will be next on show in the summer of 2020.

GERMANY

ROTHENBURG OB DER TAUBER

Many people consider Rothenburg as the nicest little town in Germany. The medieval town—with its fortified walls, old streets, and old houses restored to their original state—has been called "the marvel of the Middle Ages." Remains of the first Celtic settlement, dating back to 500 BC, have been found here. The actual village was founded in 960, and a medieval stronghold was built 10 years later, overlooking the valley of the Tauber River. At the beginning of the 12th century, King Conrad III made it an Imperial town, and an Imperial castle was built in 1140. In 1274, King Rudolf von Habsburg granted it the status of free town under the Emperor's protection. This was the beginning of a prosperous economical and cultural era. The town developed rapidly into a trading center and became one of the leading communities in Southern Germany. Rich people invested in magnificent houses; the town leaders built the City Hall and the St. George fountain; and many existing houses were redecorated. In 1356, an earthquake destroyed the two castles and many houses. The castles were replaced by public monuments or burghers' houses. By 1400, the town had a population of 6,000 people. During the Thirty Years War, Rothenburg chose the Reformist side.

The town was assailed in 1631 by the Bavarian Imperial Army led by the Count of Tilly, who was known for his cruelty, and the systematic destruction of enemy towns. Forced to surrender after a bitter fight, the town leaders presented the Count with keys to the town, and a tankard (3.26 liters) of local wine. Slightly exhilarated by the wine, Tilly said that he would spare the town and its leaders if anybody could drink the whole tankard in one draught. Mayor Nusch took the challenge, emptied the tankard, and saved his town.

This achievement (Meistertrunk, the Mayor's drink), was commemorated by a clock and a painting installed in the Councilors' Tavern, which is today the Tourist office. In 1881, this episode was adapted as a festival performance, which is nowadays shown every year on Whitsunday.

During WWII, an allied bombing destroyed the eastern part of the town, but fortunately, the historical center remained untouched. Reconstruction and restoration of the town were achieved thanks to donors from around the world, whose names are posted along the fortifications.

THINGS TO SEE OR DO IN ROTHENBURG

The Town Wall, built between 1350 and 1380, has numerous towers and several bastions. You can walk along it on the watch gangway (almost two miles) and see the plates bearing the names of the donors, many of whom are American, according to how many meters of wall they paid for.

The Hospital Bastion, on the southern-most point of the city, was completed in the 17th century. The access included seven gates with a drawbridge, and was the most heavily fortified entrance. The Klingen Bastion, another example of fortification, is located on the northern entrance. In spite of such massive defenses, the city was conquered several times.

GERMANY

The Saint George fountain, on the Market Hall square, once provided drinking water and served as a water tank in case of fire.

The City Hall is composed of two buildings, one Gothic with a belfry, guarding Herrengasse, and the other Renaissance, overlooking the Market Square.

The Councilors Tavern with the Meistertrunk (Mayor's drink) clock, is now the Tourist Office. The clock was installed in 1683, and the Meistertrunk scene was added in 1910.

Käthe Wohlfart Weihnachtsdorf This is a rather large shop with the most incredible choice of gifts and toys all related to Christmas.

EUROPE DIGEST FOR THE HURRIED TOURIST

THE RHINE

From the Gallic *renos*, meaning "river," and the Greek *rheein*, meaning "to flow," the Rhine rises in Lake Toma, Grisons Pass, Switzerland, at an altitude of 2,344 m.

An open international waterway since the Treaty of Vienna (1815), when the decision was made to suppress the 200-odd toll places, – the numerous fortresses standing on both banks of the river remind of that period – it is navigable for some 540 miles as far as Rheinfelden on the Swiss-German border.

No other river in the world has so many old and famous cities on its banks: Basel, Switzerland; Strasbourg, France; Worms, Koblenz, Mainz, Düsseldorf and Cologne, Germany; Arnhem, Holland; and industrial cities such as Duisburg, Ludwigshafen, and Leverkusen.

Water traffic is tremendous: 60,000 ships travel the river annually, transporting 60 million tons of freight, and 1,250-ton barges are increasingly being replaced by push units propelling four or six barges. Despite this traffic, and after a phase of relentless industrial development, which left the river a big dump of toxic waste, the ecological endeavors were successful, and fish have returned to Germany's main river.

In late March 1945, the U.S. Third Army under Gen. Patton began its famous bridging and crossing operations of the Rhine. Without the luck of the 9th Armored Division, who were able to capture the only intact bridge across the Rhine at Remagen, Patton's army needed to bridge the wide

GERMANY

river with their own resources. There were a total of 22 road bridges and 25 railroad bridges spanning the Rhine into Germany. With the exception of the Remagen Bridge, however, they had all been destroyed.

The first unit to cross was the fifth Infantry Division, which used assault rafts to cross the raging Rhine at Oppenheim (west of Darmstadt and south of Mainz) in the early morning hours of March 23. By March 27, despite fierce attacks by the Lufwaffe, three bridges were operational, and five divisions with supporting troops and supplies, including 40,000 vehicles, had crossed to the right bank, allowing Patton to capture Frankfurt on March 29.

GREAT BRITAIN

GREAT BRITAIN

THE NAME GREAT Britain refers to the British Isles, including England, featuring the rose as emblem, Wales, the leek, Scotland, the thistle, Northern Ireland, the clover, and smaller islands such as Jersey and Guernsey. It is part of the United Kingdom, which includes as well the overseas territories, remnant of the British Empire.

Great Britain has a population of 58 million people.

Britain is now linked to the continent by the Eurotunnel (also known as The Chunnel), which has been, and sometimes still is, considered by some Britons as an offense to their independence. The largest cities are London, Manchester, and Birmingham in England; Glasgow and Edinburgh in Scotland; Cardiff in Wales; and Belfast in Northern Ireland. The United Kingdom is the oldest constitutional monarchy in the world, founded in the 9th century, but it has no constitution as such: it is ruled by a tradition of laws, the first one being the Great Chart (the Magna Carta) adopted in 1215. Elizabeth II (born Elizabeth Alexandra Mary on April 21, 1926) is the Queen regnant

EUROPE DIGEST FOR THE HURRIED TOURIST

of 16 independent sovereign states known informally as the Commonwealth realms: the United Kingdom, Canada, Australia, New Zealand, Jamaica, Barbados, the Bahamas, Grenada, Papua New Guinea, the Solomon Islands, Tuvalu, Saint Lucia, Saint Vincent and the Grenadines, Belize, Antigua and Barbuda, and Saint Kitts and Nevis. In 2002, the U.K. celebrated the Queen's jubilee. Before her, only George III and Queen Victoria had achieved such a long reign. Nobody knows the exact amount of her personal fortune. The last estimations ranked her 105th among the richest people in the world, with a fortune of €1.8 billion, including her personal belongings, various collections, paintings, and jewels. The income from the estates owned by the crown is today paid to the state, which allows the Queen a yearly alimony of €13 million, plus expenses for travel, maintenance of the Royal palaces, and the wages of the some 300 people at her service. The Queen officially rules the kingdom, but she does not participate in the government. Her Majesty's government, also known as "The Crown", represents her (although the Queen must still approve some important acts personally).

The Parliament has two chambers. The upper chamber is the House of Lords. It is composed of bishops holding a see in England, judges of the High Courts, nobles, and hereditary peers, which can examine, discuss and amend projects of laws, but cannot refuse the laws passed by the Cabinet of Ministers. By provision of the House of Lords Act, hereditary peers (then 750) were deprived of their 700 year-old privilege to sit and vote in the upper chamber. A

GREAT BRITAIN

compromise allowed 92 of them, elected by their fellow peers, to remain as temporary members, plus 75 peers elected by their party groups. The number of Lords has thus been reduced from more than 1,000 to 670.

The lower chamber of Parliament is called the House of Commons. It is composed of 650 democratically elected members, known as MPs (members of Parliament), and has legislative powers.

"Rule Britannia!"

"Rule, Britannia!" is a British patriotic song, originating from the poem "Rule, Britannia" by James Thomson and set to music by Thomas Arne in 1740. Today, this message might well not be true anymore, as Britain's domination has suffered from the loss of its colonies, the industrial competition from low-wages countries, and the economic crisis, However, as far back as the Renaissance in the 15th century and until the end of WWII, Britain has overpowered the world, not only in the military field, but also in science, literature, art, banking, and engineering.

FAMOUS BRITISH ACHIEVEMENTS

Science: By 1700, there was a commitment to science as the firm basis for success in commerce and industry. Britain's rapid industrialisation over the next century and its domination of world trade confirmed the importance of science in driving the economy.

It is to Bacon that we owe the development of British science in 17th century. Sir Francis Bacon (1561-1626), often called the 'Father' of modern science, made no major scientific discoveries himself, but wrote extensively on empirical scientific methods.

In 1675 the Royal Observatory was established at Greenwich.

Among those closely associated with charting the heavens over the next 25 years were Edmond Halley (1656-1742) and Sir Isaac Newton (1642-1727).

17th century advances in microscopy, medicine, chemistry and biology have probably been as important as Newton's laws of motion, and the development of precision instruments placed Britain in the forefront of specialist equipment making.

Francis and Roger Bacon, George Berkeley (Philosophy), Edmond Halley (Astronomy), Isaac Newton, Michael Faraday (Physics), Alexander Fleming (1945 Nobel prize for his works on antibiotics, leading to the discovery of penicillin), Ronald Ross (1902 Nobel prize for his work on malaria), are amongst the greatest names in this field.

Literature: English descends from the language spoken by the north Germanic tribes who settled in England from the 5th century A.D. onwards.

The earliest written works in Old English (as scholars now know their language) were probably composed orally at first.

From 1066 onwards, the language is Middle English, and the first great name in English literature is that of Geoffrey Chaucer (1343-1400).

With the invention of the printing press by Jonannes

GREAT BRITAIN

Gutenberg around 1440, and the mechanization of bookmaking, literature developed rapidly. Many authors appeared, that were to make British literature perhaps the world's greatest.

No other country in the world has so many poets. Amongst the multitude of authors, the following are never to be forgotten:

Edmund Spenser (1552-1599), Sir Walter Raleigh (1552-1618), Christopher Marlowe (1564-1593), William Shakespeare (1564-1616), John Milton (1608-1674), Alexander Pope (1688-1744), William Wordsworth (1770-1850), Samuel Taylor Coleridge (1772-1834), Robert Burns (1759 1796) – after Shakespeare, Burns is perhaps the most often quoted of writers in English: we sing his Auld Lang Syne every New Year's Eve, – John Keats (1795-1821), Percy Shelley (1792-1822; husband of Mary Shelley), George Gordon, Lord Byron (1788-1824), Alfred, Lord Tennyson (1809-1892) and Robert Browning (1812-1889), W.B. (William Butler) Yeats (1865-1939, T.S. (Thomas Stearns) Eliot (1888-1965).

The field of prose fiction and novels cannot be forgotten, with great writers such as Jonathan Swift (1667-1745), best-known for Gulliver's Travels, Daniel Defoe (1661-1731), author of Robinson Crusoe and Moll Flanders, Sir Walter Scott (1771-1832) and Jane Austen (1775-1817), Mary Shelley (1797-1851), famous for her Frankenstein, Charles Dickens (1812-1870), Charlotte Brontë (1816-1855) and her sisters Emily (1818-1848) and Anne (1820-1849), R.L. Stevenson (1850-94) writer of The Strange Case of Dr.

EUROPE DIGEST FOR THE HURRIED TOURIST

Jekyll and Mr. Hyde, Rudyard Kipling (1865-1936), George Bernard Shaw (1856-1950), H.G. Wells (1866-1946), John Galsworthy (1867-1933), E.M. Forster (1879-1970), James Joyce (1882-1941), Virginia Woolf (1882-1941), D.H. Lawrence (1885-1930), George Orwell (1903-50), Graham Greene (1904-1991)

Music: Henry Purcell, Edward Elgar, Benjamin Britten, The Beatles, The Rolling Stones

Painting: The history of British painting is intimately linked with the broader traditions of European painting. Kings and queens commissioned portraits from German, Dutch, and Flemish artists. British painters found inspiration and guidance from these continental masters, and from their journeys abroad, in Italy especially.

Beginning in the early eighteenth century, English artists began to develop their own styles in marine and allegorical painting. The great flowering of English landscape painting came during the first half of the nineteenth century. If one drew up a list of British painters, almost fifty names would appear in the 18th century, and more than 125 in the 19th.

Let us simply remember the five greatest ones:

William Hogarth (1697-1764)
Sir Joshua Reynolds (1723-1792)
Thomas Gainsborough (1727-1788)
John Constable (1776-1837)
William Turner (1775-1851)

GREAT BRITAIN

British people love sports: soccer, rugby, cricket, golf, polo, car racing – some of the leading racing cars are designed by the British, such as McLaren. They are also fond of animals, mainly horses (one says that when a lady riding her horse in Hyde Park dismounted as her horse stumbled, a few passersby helped the lady, and 25 rushed to the horse), vintage cars, and of course, new ones like Rolls Royce, Bentley, Rover, Jaguar, Cooper, M.G., etc.

They enjoy military parades such as Trooping the Colors in London, and the Tattoo in Edinburgh, very refined clubs – some of which still refuse female members –, standing or sitting for hours in pubs, and drinking pints of ale, or lager beer (which became popular after WWII). The British invented rugby football, modern tennis, golf, seaside resorts, the telephone, railways, the stamp, the greeting card, tweed clothing, and income tax.

Malt whisky is a Scottish contribution (some say it is Irish), along with the kilt, the national dress of the Highlanders of Scotland. The kilt is a skirt made of tartan, a checkered or cross-barred species of cloth. Each clan of Scotland has its own pattern.

They also invented the subway: the first underground line opened in 1863, and the first tube line opened in 1866. Subsequent lines of the network were built under the supervision of Charles Tyson Yerkes, an American railway magnate. The British are fierce traditionalists and cling to ceremonies that would seem ridiculous anywhere else: the "beefeaters" guarding the Tower of London, Scots clad with kilts, the uniforms at Eton High school, the bowler

EUROPE DIGEST FOR THE HURRIED TOURIST

hat, etc. Somehow, Brits never look ridiculous, mainly perhaps because of their sense of honor, pride, and bravery. Great Britain was never invaded again after William the Conqueror's famous victory over King Harold's English Army in Hastings on October 14, 1066. This explains why the country contains so many castles, cathedrals, churches, and mansion houses, some of which were built as far back as the 10th century. For instance, the Tower of London was achieved in 1078. Great Britain is also the place for exclusive clothing: exceptional shoes, tweed jackets, lamb's wool or cashmere pullovers, trench coats, and raincoats from Burberry's, Aquascutum, Barbour, etc. There is a definite type of British elegance, which foreigners fail sometimes to understand. For instance, an elegant gentleman will buy a brand new expensive tweed jacket, stuff its pockets with stones, and hang it outside in the rain until it reaches the shape of a floor cloth.

The British rarely shake hands, except when they are first introduced. When greeted with a "How do you do?" the correct response is, "How do you do?" When asked, "How are you?" a polite response is, "Very well, thank you." Social conversations usually center on the weather (an essential subject), sport, animals, or holidays. To talk about your health, personal feelings/beliefs, politics, or death is considered bad taste. Discussions of cooking are considered as boring, although some daily TV broadcasts on cooking become more and more popular, as are books on the subject. In fact, cooking well has become the mark of a perfect host and a token of savoir-vivre.

GREAT BRITAIN

At the table, the English rest their hands in their lap. You should not touch your knife or fork before the last person is served. Both hands are use to cut and eat; the fork never passes from the left to right hand, as is often the case in America. The English love gathering in pubs, clubs, and Old students' associations. They also have a certain liking for uniforms: school dresses, college scarves, club ties, clan kilts for Scots and Irish. The Brits are great snobs but, unlike the French who strive to adopt the latest possible gimmick, they are conservative, and their snobbism consists of respecting traditional attitudes, customs, and a certain lifestyle.

EUROPE DIGEST FOR THE HURRIED TOURIST

LONDON

With a population of 7.5 million inhabitants, London covers an enormous area of 600 sq. mi. and includes 33 boroughs, former villages that still keep their names: Westminster, Chelsea, Holborn, Greenwich, Paddington, etc. London receives more than 15 million foreign visitors a year.

The city is one of the world's greatest financial centers and home to 539 foreign banks and 300,000 employees. London is also a major center for fashion and entertainment. Edition and printing are the most important sectors with 12 press editors and 14 million buyers.

London was settled by the Romans in 50AD around a wooden bridge built across the Thames River, in a place called Lyn-Din (Celtic name for "Lake Stronghold") and named therefore Londinium. It was believed that the Romans built the bridge, but recent research proved that the bridge and the surrounding settlement existed in 700 BC.

In 1066, the year of the Norman invasion, London covered an area of one square mile, which is today the City. After his victory, William the Conqueror crowned himself king in the newly built Westminster Abbey. He then ordered the construction of the Tower of London. The city grew to become a trading center and a bustling medieval metropolis. Henry VIII, with his colorful character and his headstrong lifestyle, went into conflict with the Church, broke relations with the Pope, dissolved the monasteries,

GREAT BRITAIN

and confiscated Church property. The result was a boom on the real estate market, which spurred new expansion for London. Henry collected palaces the way he collected wives (he had six in all). When his daughter, Elizabeth I, sat on the throne, Britain entered a glorious golden age. After being been hit by the Plague in 1665, Tudor London was practically destroyed by the Great Fire of 1666. Over 13,000 buildings and 87 churches went up in smoke. Many Londoners moved to the country, and city limits exploded. The West End extended as far as Richmond, where many people built houses to get away from the smells of Central London. An ambitious rebuilding program proposed by John Nash followed. Construction of St. Paul's Cathedral by Christopher Wren was the crowning achievement. The next great era for London was the conquest of the empire, which covered one-fifth of the globe and brought wealth and prosperity. The reign of Queen Victoria from 1837 to 1901was the summit of this glorious period..

Everyday's life was not easy for the city population. Let's try to imagine how London looks in 1700:

The city is a bustling metropolis, which no European capital can match in size or vigor. Building is going on everywhere. Dominating the landscape is Wren's incomplete masterpiece, St Paul, its dome still covered with scaffolding. It has a population of 530,000, one-ninth of the entire English population. The second largest city, Norwich, has only 30,000 inhabitants. Every year, more than 8,000 young people pour into London, attracted by the promise of wages twice that of anywhere else. Aristocracy and gentry come to

EUROPE DIGEST FOR THE HURRIED TOURIST

be seen at the Court, to settle their legal affairs, to arrange marriage for their children, or to shop.

For rich people, London is a shopper's paradise. The choice is enormous, offering the best of European merchandize and goods from the remotest parts of the world. However, London is also a place of disease and criminality. Its stink is terrible. The streets are open sewers. The water is undrinkable, and the death rate is much higher than the birth rate. One-third of all newborn children die within 2 years and one half live to age 15. In polite society, women withdraw after dinner to give men the privacy to drink port and use the chamber pots, which are kept handy in a special compartment (the French word *lieu d'aisance* has just entered the language, still surviving today in the shortened loo). The sewage is kept in the basement until picked-up by the night soil collectors. Even so, many streets are full of human waste, and pedestrians are obliged to walk in the middle of the road to avoid being drenched by the contents of chamber pots emptied from upstairs windows. They can also expect to be harassed by hungry dogs, beggars, and young women who have travelled from the country seeking fortune. At night, men carry swords to ward off muggers. Foreign visitors are often struck by the Englishman's capacity for alcohol, a side effect of the filthy water. Morals are lax: around 10 percent of women are pregnant on their wedding day, and clerics complain about the prevalence of premarital sex. Contraception is almost unknown. Condoms, made of sheep's intestines, are imported from France (hence the name "French leathers"). They must be tied on with red rib-

GREAT BRITAIN

bons. Venereal disease is rife and syphilis endemic, to the point that it is called the "London disease." Brothels flourish, particularly in Covent Garden, where a prostitute can be had for as little as half a crown—although better establishments charge far higher prices. However, many other delights await the traveler. For instance, one French visitor was bemused by the Englishman's capacity to consume vast quantities of roast beef but overwhelmed by admiration for the English pudding.

Hundred years later, things started to change, as people poured into London in search of work. Property speculators bought enormous areas of land around the city, erecting miles of cramped, terraced houses. Infrastructure, from the underground to the sewers, followed, and is still in use today.. Urbanization spread all over the numerous villages around London, which became city suburbs with curvy narrow streets choked with traffic at rush hours. After WWI, the elegant mansions of the West End were split up into apartments, symbolizing the disintegration of the British Empire and society. During WWII, the Luftwaffe flattened large areas of constructions in the center of London, and the reconstruction after the war saw the replacement of the village-like terraced houses by inhuman tower blocks and metal-glass office skyscrapers, which are now images of Central London. Traditions play an important role in London life. They include the changing of the guard at Buckingham Palace, the changing of the horse guards, trooping the colors on Queen's anniversary day, the Lord Mayor's procession through the city in a golden state coach on the second Saturday in November.

Taxis

There are 23,000 taxis in London. The London taxis, called cabs, generally black, and their drivers have earned the reputation for providing the best taxi service in the world.

The cab that most people associate with London taxis is the Austin FX-4, introduced in 1959. The model, with many modifications over the years, remained in production until 1997, making it one of the longest running production vehicles in history.

Their famous 25 ft turning circle means that they can turn "on a sixpence" (or a dime). All taxis can carry five people plus luggage. Black cabs are the only taxis allowed to apply for hire in London. Drivers are required to pass a daunting exam known as "The Knowledge" before they can sit behind the wheel. The Knowledge takes two years of study; prospective drivers must memorize some 25,000 streets near Central London and learn the quickest way between points. They must also know the whereabouts of every hospital, theater, hotel, train station, etc. They sit for months of rigorous exams before being certified.

They know London so well that they manage somehow to avoid traffic jams (although not always) and never have a problem taking you to even the tiniest street or lane in the city. Taxis are a good option for groups sharing the fare, which can be steep—the meter starts ticking at £1.40 and rises by 20p with every 219 m travelled. Be aware that

GREAT BRITAIN

evening rates are more expensive, with a 60p surcharge kicking in at 8pm, up to 90p after midnight. Tipping at about 10% is expected.

Note that it can be difficult to hail a cab in popular tourist or nightclub areas, and drivers are perfectly within their rights to refuse a fare, especially if they suspect intoxication. You can phone Radio Taxis at 7272 0272 to order a cab, but you'll pay an extra £1.20.

The Underground (Subway)

The best and fastest way to get around town is the subway, called the Underground or the Tube, and is the most extensive underground railway network in the world. It serves London Town as well as a large part of Greater London and neighboring areas of Essex, Hertfordshire, and Buckinghamshire.

The Underground has 270 stations and about 250 miles of track. In 2007, more than one billion passenger journeys were recorded, making it the third busiest metro system in Europe after Paris and Moscow. The Tube map, with its schematic non-geographical layout and color-coded lines, is considered a design classic; many other transport maps worldwide have been influenced by it.

Buses

Another way is to travel on a red "double-decker" — the unmistakable image of the London bus. The charm of sitting on the upper deck of the London buses 5 m above street level is always worth the voyage. London's bus network is one of the largest in the world, running 24 hours a day, with 8,000 buses, 700 bus routes, and over 6 million passenger journeys made every weekday. Their frequency and the tight mesh of bus stops make moving around town very easy.

A single journey costs £4 on the Underground, and £2 on the Bus, which might prove to be quite expensive if you use London transport several times during the day. For one-day travel, the Oyster Card can be purchased upon arrival or even in advance through Internet: www.tfl.gov.uk (delivery time to U.S. 7 to 12 days). Such cards are valid for the Tube and on buses within city limits. They also entitle you to a discount on the river boats fares.

If you are travelling as an individual and want to see several places, monuments or museums, a good solution is to buy a London pass with travel: a three-day card costs £90 and provides free access on the Underground and buses as well as to the majority of monuments, museums and Thames river cruises with priority entrance (see www.londonpass.com).

Sightseeing double-deckers are also to be found everywhere: the round trip, valid the whole day, costs from 13 to 15 £, but you enjoy riding in an open-roof bus, and can jump off-jump on wherever and as many times as you like.

SOME FACTS ABOUT LONDON

- In October 2009, it had an official population of 7,556,900 within the boundaries of Greater London.

GREAT BRITAIN

- One in eight of the UK population lives in London.
- A huge 47.3% of London's population is aged 16 to 44.
- 40% of London's total population belongs to ethnic minority groups.
- There are 33 different communities of more than 10,000 members born overseas in the town and its surroundings, and more than 200 languages are spoken.
- London has 23,000 Licensed Taxis.
- There are over 12,000 restaurants and 5,400 pubs and bars.
- London's restaurant and café culture encompasses cuisines from over 70 different countries worldwide.
- London is home to 123 historic buildings and monuments and 33 historic gardens.
- London has over 200 museums, 600 cinemas, 108 music halls, and 3 approved country parks.
- There are 95 golf courses, 50 athletics tracks, 2,000 tennis courts, 7 ice rinks, 546 swimming pools, 37 rowing clubs, 12 professional football teams, 2 county cricket clubs, and 6 race courses, all within one hour of London.
- London has 1,500 drama groups, 600 dance groups, and 5 symphony orchestras.
- London attracts 15 million international visitors per year, making it the world's second most visited city after Paris.
- The population of London is forecasted to rise from 7.4 million to 8.1 million people by 2016 – this is a population increase equivalent to a city the size of Leeds.

- At least 23,000 new homes are built annually.
- In 2008, it was anticipated that 636,000 new jobs would be created over the next 15 years, but the 2009 crisis lowered this figure by half.

WHAT TO DO OR VISIT IN LONDON

CHANGING OF THE GUARD

This is a colorful display of pageantry by the Queen's personal guard and the Foot Guard of the Army. It takes place daily at 11:30am between Buckingham Palace and Wellington Barracks.

TOWER OF LONDON

Tower Hill, EC3 Tube: Tower Hill 020 7709 0765

Home of the famous Beefeaters, officially named "Her Majesty's Royal Palace and Fortress" but more commonly known as "The Tower," it is a historic fortress which has also been used as a prison, a place of execution and torture, an armory, a treasury, a zoo, the Royal Mint, a public records office, and, since 1303, the home of the Crown Jewels of the United Kingdom. It is the oldest building used by the British government.

BRITISH MUSEUM

Great Russell Square. Tube: Holborn, Tottenham Court Road, Russell Square

britishmuseum.org.uk

GREAT BRITAIN

The British Museum holds seven million exhibits that display artifacts from ancient Egypt, Greece, Rome, etc. Admission is free.

NATIONAL GALLERY
Trafalgar square
nationalgallery.org.uk

It houses a rich collection of over 2,300 paintings dating from the mid-13th century to 1900.

THE LONDON EYE Jubilee Gardens, South Bank, SE1 Tube: Waterloo 0870 500 0600

Also known as the Millenium Wheel, it is the largest Ferris wheel in Europe (443 ft high) and the world's third highest observation wheel after Singapore (541 ft) and Nanchang, China (525 ft). The complete rotation takes 30 minutes. It has become the most popular paid tourist attraction in the United Kingdom, visited by over three million people each year.

TRAFALGAR SQUARE

A favorite gathering place for Londoners and visitors, it is over-topped by the famous column and statue of Horatio Nelson, one of the greatest heroes of English history. The name commemorates the Battle of Trafalgar (1805), a British naval victory of the Napoleonic Wars.

EUROPE DIGEST FOR THE HURRIED TOURIST

Horatio Nelson, Viscount

Horatio, Lord Nelson, was the most celebrated admiral in British history. Born on September 29, 1758, he entered the Royal Navy in 1770 at the age of 12 and was a captain by 1778.

Nelson played a distinguished part in the defeat of the Spanish fleet off Cape Saint Vincent in 1797. The following year, he achieved one of his most brilliant and crushing victories in the Battle of the Nile. Finding the French fleet in the Bay of Abukir, he adopted the adventurous and unexpected tactic of maneuvering part of his fleet from the shore side, putting the French line of ships under cross fire. Stationed next at Naples he began a celebrated liaison with Emma, Lady Hamilton, wife of the British ambassador; she bore him a daughter in 1801. At the Battle of Copenhagen in 1801, Nelson put a telescope to his blind eye – he had been blinded in battle in 1794 and lost his right arm in 1797 – to avoid seeing a signal from his commander, Sir Hyde Parker, ordering him to retreat.

Upon the renewal of war with France in 1803, Nelson was given the crucial task of blockading the French fleet at Toulon. Although he failed to prevent the French from breaking out and uniting with the Spanish fleet in 1805, he eventually brought the combined navies to battle. Nelson had 27 ships under his command. He broke through the French–Spanish fleet of 33 ships and captured 17 of them, destroying the others. His words before the battle have become famous: "England expects that every man will do his duty." He was killed in the battle, but he lived long enough

GREAT BRITAIN

to know that his victory was complete. The Victory, his flagship at Trafalgar, is preserved at Portsmouth.

TATE MODERN GALLERY
Bankside, SE1 020 78 87 80 00
tate.org.uk/modern
Located in an old power station, this gallery offers a wide variety of modern art from Picasso, Matisse, Mondrian, Dali, Bacon, Pollock, Rothko, Warhol, and more.

CABINET WAR ROOMS
Clive Steps, King Charles St. Tube: Westminster 0171 930 69 61
This labyrinth of 21 underground rooms was used as the secret headquarters of the British Government from 1939 to 1945.

MADAME TUSSAUD'S
Marylebone Road, NW1 Tube: Baker Street 0870 400 3s
World-famous collection of wax figures

HMS BELFAST. 0171 940 6328 Tube: Tower Bridge or London Bridge Entrance from Tooley St.
Europe's only surviving armored warship from WWII

ROYAL AIR FORCE MUSEUM HENDON
Grahame Park Way, London NW9 SLL Tube: Colindale (Northern Line) – Rail: Mill Hill Broadway 0891 6005 633
This exhibition displays over 70 full-sized aircraft , in-

cluding a unique collection of British and German planes.

HAMPTON COURT PALACE
0181 781 9500
By Train: 32 min. Direct from Waterloo to Hampton Court. By River Launch: from Westminster Pier. By Tube: Richmond, then Bus R68
hrp.org.uk/hamptoncourtpalace
The oldest Tudor palace in England, this was Henry VIII's favorite residence.

WINDSOR CASTLE
Windsor, Berkshire 01753 868286
windsor.gov.uk
Rail: Windsor & Eton Central/Windsor & Eton Riverside
One of the oldest and largest medieval castles in the world, it has been built after the Norman invasion by William the Conqueror. It has been the home of the Royal Family for over 900 years, and is the Queen's preferred weekend home.

TRIPS ON RIVER THAMES
Campion Launches – Catamaran Cruises – Circular Cruises – City Cruises – Thames Cruises – Thames Leisure – Turk Launches.

From Embankment Pier (tube: Embankment), Tower Millennium Pier (tube: Tower Hill), Waterloo Millennium Pier (tube: Waterloo), Westminster Millennium Pier (tube: Waterloo). No need to book in advance, although this would save time lining up for tickets.

GREAT BRITAIN

This is a must-do thing for the first-time London visitor. You get great views of London from the river, and the commentary provides interesting information.

SHOPPING

London is meant for shopping. For instance, the 1.5 miles of Oxford Street are completely lined with shops .

The low rate of the British pound to the American dollar, together with the V.A.T. refund scheme for exports to U.S., allow the customer to profit from affordable prices.

The fame of British fashion is undisputable. Names like Burberry, Aquascutum and Barbour for outdoor luxury clothing, Austin Reed for men's and women's contemporary dressing, Pringle for lamb's wool and cashmere garments, Church's and Clarks for shoes, do not need to be introduced.

The best is to shop for these garments directly at the designer's original store, where the latest models can be found in all sizes. However, large department stores such as Harrod's and Selfridges offer a wide range of products from many designers, enabling the customer to browse around different stands.

Britain artisanship also excels in many other fields:

- China from Royal Doulton, Wedgewood, or Royal Worcester,
- Guns and accessories from Holland & Holland (if you are a true hunter and can afford a five to six figures check for a double-barrel gun, this is the place),

- Brass accessories, from door knobs to bell shaped weights, antique and modern silver (the Silver Vaults in Chancery Lane are a must to visit — it is the world's largest retail collection of silver artifacts. Thousands of silver objects are on display, from a Champagne swizzle stick to a full size silver armchair),
- Exquisite English furniture such as Chesterfield sofas or Captain Chairs, etc.

The main shopping area is a perimeter in the center of London delimited by Oxford Street to the North, Regent Street, and Piccadilly Circus to the East, Jermyn Street to the South, and further to South-West Knightsbridge area and Brompton Road.

The visit should definitely start at Harrod's on Brompton Road. Initiated as a small shop by Charles Henri Harrod in 1894, the present building was constructed in 1905. This is a British institution. Today, it is owned by Mohamed Al Fayed, father of Dodi Al Fayed, who died with Princess Diana in a car crash in 1997. Harrod's is one of the largest department stores in the world. More than 5,000 staff from 50 different countries work in the 330 departments and the 17 restaurants.

The second largest department store in the UK is Selfridges on Oxford Street. Less flamboyant than Harrods, it is recommended for the variety and quality of its assortment.

Between Oxford Street and Piccadilly, the area covering Bond Street, Conduit Street, South Molton Street, and

Savile Row is much praised for its exclusive luxury fashion shops, jewelers, custom-made shoes, hair salons, and traditional English tailors. Many of them are granted a warrant of supplier to the Court of England.

Shoppers might purchase a useful shopping guide, the Street sensation London street guide, which lists all shopping areas and streets in central London. This 40-page leaflet costs $12 if posted to Europe and $16 worlwide Delivery is three days to Europe, five elsewhere; it is possible to ask for delivery to your hotel.

It can be ordered on Internet:
streetsensation.co.uk/theguide/theguide.htm

STROLLING

PORTOBELLO ROAD

The flea market on Saturdays is worth visiting. Portobello Road also offers many antique bookstores, open all weak.

COVENT GARDEN MARKET

Formerly the central fruit and vegetables market of London and the city's first planned square, the covered halls of the market were transformed in 1970 into a lively compound of smart shops, cafes and restaurants, which are busy at all times.

SOHO

In the 1970s, Soho was the capital's red light district.

EUROPE DIGEST FOR THE HURRIED TOURIST

New restaurants, bars and clubs, as well as hippie and punk fashion boutiques, have now become popular.

HYDE PARK SPEAKER'S CORNER

Located on the corner of Park Lane and Oxford Street, opposite Marble Arch tube station, the Speakers' Corner is the spiritual home of the British democratic tradition of soapbox oratory. People from all walks of life gather to listen to speeches about anything and everything – and to heckle. From Socialism to Sunday trading, sausages to space invaders, the opinions aired here are varied and fascinating. Karl Marx, Lenin, George Orwell, and William Morris have all used this spot to express their ideals. Today, the average speakers are not quite as high profile, and their coherence also varies greatly, but as a whole, it makes for great street theater. Although Sunday morning is the best time to visit, speakers can now be found on the corner throughout the week.

LONDON GUIDED WALKS 020 7624 3978

London walks are an original way to discover the hidden and secret parts of London

GREAT BRITAIN

WHERE TO EAT

Food from the whole world is offered in this cosmopolitan city: Italian, Indian, Pakistani, Chinese, French, Greek, and Jewish restaurants abound. Fast-food joints flourish, too, but they are not of the same quality as in the U.S. and should be avoided unless in a great hurry. At the lunch hour, English workers often eat their sandwiches while walking or riding on the bus or the underground.

Until not so long ago, it was difficult to find edible cuisine in Great Britain. Staying as a French lecturer in Birmingham in the late 1950s, I remember having to show the local butcher how to cut out fillets of beef. Besides the traditional fish and chips, beef and kidney pie, cooked York ham, roast beef, and stews, the best English cooking at that time was in fact Indian, Pakistani, or Italian. Today, one of the most popular dishes in England is still Indian: *chicken tikka masala*.

Even today, among the 50 best restaurants in the world ranked by the Restaurant Magazine, only four are British.

Under the influence of the growing number of foreign visitors, things began to change, and grilled meat became popular. Green peas no longer looked or tasted like small table-tennis balls. The Italians introduced the use of olive oil and tasty tomato preparations. The brown watery mixture called coffee gave way to espresso and cappuccino. Recently, Jamie Oliver has done a lot to promote good cooking, and he is certainly the master of the Anglo-continental cuisine resurgence.

EUROPE DIGEST FOR THE HURRIED TOURIST

Ramsay's Kitchen Nightmares, a television program featuring British celebrity chef Gordon Ramsay visiting a failing restaurant and acting to improve the establishment in just one week, helped as well raising the quality and standard of British cuisine.

Today, it is possible to eat reasonably well in about 30% of the 12,000 restaurants in London. However, I will not take the risk to recommend any place. Eating in a pub is inexpensive and provides a good look at the British way of life. Many pubs offer simple English food of good quality. Less conspicuous and fussy than their fellows restaurateurs, some pub owners offer simple, and sometimes excellent, catering at fair prices, offering pork pies, steak and kidney pies, various types of salads, excellent cooked ham, and more elaborate stews. Some of them have kept their 18th or 19th century decoration, and offer a cultural heritage with a lot of atmosphere. Here is my personal selection of worthwhile pubs in London.

Location Hyde Park Corner

The Grenadier

18 Wilton Row SW1 Tube: Hyde Park Corner

Featuring military decoration, it offers good beer and fine traditional cooking.

Location Covent Garden

Lamb & Flag (formerly named the Bucket of Blood)

33 Rose Street WC2 Tube: Covent Garden or Leicester Square

Built in 1623, this is practically the last remaining

wooden-frame building in London and one of the most charming pubs in the West End.

Location Kensington High Street
Churchill Arms

119 Kensington High Street W8 Tube: Kensington High Street or Notting Hill Gate

Often mentioned in tourist guidebooks, this pub has every inch of wall and ceiling covered with photos, posters, brass jugs, chamber pots, butterflies, and souvenirs related to Winston Churchill. Service is first class. Asian waitresses serve Thai food.

Location Soho
Argyll Arms

18 Argyll Street W1 Tube: Oxford Circus Opened in 1866, it has retained its classy Victorian mirrors and mahogany decoration, apparently unchanged since 19th century.. The restaurant is acceptable, and the central location (right by the Oxford Circus tube station) makes it a favorite joint for office clerks and executives working in the area. Location Fleet Street, Blackfriars and St Paul's

Old Bank of London

194 Fleet Street EC4 Tube: Chancery Lane or Temple

Just nearby the Courts of Justice, this is former bank features an impressive hall with marble and brass and a balcony ringing the central bar. There are 31 beer hand pumps.

EUROPE DIGEST FOR THE HURRIED TOURIST

Ye Olde Cheshire Cheese
145 Fleet Street EC4 Tube: Blackfriars
Just like the 17th century taverns of popular imagination, it's a warren of narrow corridors and myriad rooms, including three restaurants. Thackeray used to booze here, and Dickens mentions it in "A Tale of Two Cities."

Punch Tavern 99 Fleet Street EC4 Tube: Blackfriars The famous satirical magazine of the same name was founded here in 1841. Amid the extravagant Victorian decor, which was brilliantly refurbished, many of Punch's ancient cartoons line the walls as well as stacks of Punch and Judy curios.

Location Wapping
Prospect of Whitby
57 Wapping Wall E1 Tube: Wapping
Built in 1520 and remodeled in 1777, this historic pub is a tourist attraction. Dickens, Samuel Pepys, and Dr. Johnson drank here. The 230-year old decor has been miraculously preserved, while the river views from the terrace and balcony are well worth a look. The restaurant upstairs serves pricey fish and roast dishes.

Location Docklands
Dickens Inn
St Katherine's way E1 Tube: Tower Hill
In the middle of the reconstructed dockland area, this is a huge warehouse transformed into a three-story building with five separate bars and restaurants, including a pizzeria

and a fish restaurant. In the summer, customers can flood the large outside sitting with the view on the marina.

THE THAMES RIVER

The name "Thames" comes from the Sanskrit *tamas*, which means "dark water." Indeed, the waters are dark, not only in appearance but also in terms of their history. London has always been a city where to die was easier than to survive, and the Thames has greatly contributed to increase the death toll. On the evening of September 1348 in the harbor of London, after a day of usual activity loading and unloading ships moored along the quays, the rats infesting the ships ran ashore and subsequently changed the course of English history. These rats carried the Bubonic Plague or Black Death, which spread rapidly along the riverbanks and covered the whole country like a toxic cloud. From the 1.5 million English population, 500,000 died. The Black Death remained at an endemic stage until the end of the 17th century. Today, the Thames has lost much of its commercial function. The port activity has moved down to the estuary, and Londoners are reconciled with their River. It hasn't always been the case: for a very long time, London ignored and despised what it would not accept but as a necessary nuisance. The River was once called The Great Stink: all the effluents of the city were poured directly into the River, where the drinking water was also pumped. There was only one bridge to cross the river: the London Bridge. It was always packed. In 1212, the bridge, covered with houses built in wood, burned down; 3,000 died in the fire. The South Bank was just a miserable suburb with the Bank side Red Light district where prostitution and gambling prevailed, but also theaters –including the famous Shakespeare Globe theater. In 1858, the stink of the River became so insufferable that the Parliament had to move away from their premises. Disraeli, then Chancellor, decided to build a network of sewers along the river to take the pestilence further down. For esthetic reasons, the sewers were covered, and embankments were built on the River sides. During the 18th and 19th centuries, hundreds of thousands of immigrants, mainly Irish and Jews, came to London and settled in sordid conditions in the East End, near the docks and the slaughterhouses. They paid a heavy tribute to the Thames: 140,000 died of cholera, typhoid, and dysentery between 1830 and 1860. There were periods of remission only when the Thames froze, which was common until the 20th century. The East End became a place of depravity, where members of good society used to come and quiver at the sight of people living like animals. As the prisons on land and on floating barges filled up, Parliament sent these populations to the newly born colonies, mainly Australia. Today, practically nothing is left from the docks. Burnt out when the German incendiary bombs fell on barges containing coal, oil and other inflammable materials, they remained empty until the 1970s, when an ambitious program started reconstructing the whole area. Modern buildings were erected around marinas or along the river. At first, no one wanted to live there, and flats were difficult to sell. Today, the price for a one-person studio is more than £200,000, for a penthouse, around £4 million.

New projects range from £600 to £950 per square foot. Canary Wharf, a project supported by Mrs. Thatcher, has become a major banking and business area. Katharina's Wharf is a lively marina, with shops and restaurants.

CANTERBURY AND DOVER

Canterbury has always attracted visitors, from the pilgrims described by Chaucer in "Canterbury's Tales" to the present tourists. The Romans began the first settlement in 43 AD, but it was the arrival of Saint Augustine that put Canterbury at the heart of English history. When he baptized King Ethelbert in 597, the king gave him a church. Sacked by Danish invaders in 1023, restored under King Canute, it was rebuilt as a cathedral under the Normans in the 11th and 12th centuries. It was here that Archbishop Thomas Becket was murdered in 1170 by four knights who took for an order the famous wish of the king Henry II: "Will no one rid me of that turbulent priest?" He was buried in the Cathedral. Soon after the death of Thomas Becket, Pope Alexander canonized him and the murdered priest was elevated to sainthood. Becket's shrine at Canterbury then became the most important place in the country for pilgrims to visit, and the third Christian destination after Jerusalem and Rome. When Henry VIII broke with Rome, Canterbury Cathedral became the mother church of new Anglicanism, and the king had Becket's shrine destroyed in 1538. It is recorded that 26 wagonloads of gold, silver, jewels, and other valuables were stolen from the shrine and taken to the tower of London to be added to the king's treasury. Today at Canterbury cathedral, a candle is kept lit to mark the former site of the shrine, but nothing else remains.

Dover Castle Built in the 11th century, the castle is one of the largest fortifications in the country, strategically located at the shortest crossing point to continental Europe. The castle, and its network of tunnels going deep within Dover's famous White Cliffs, was used during WWII as an underground hospital, and headquarters for Vice Admiral Ramsay and Winston Churchill during Operation Dynamo, when 388,000 troops were evacuated from Dunkirk.

ITALY

ITALY

AREA: 117,490 sq.mi. Population: 57 million people Shaped like a boot, Italy runs 808 miles long from north to south and has a great variety of landscapes and climates. Its 5,000 miles of coast, sunny climate, delicious food and wines, archeological heritage, Renaissance architecture, painters, and musicians attract more than 21 million annual visitors, more than 2 million of which are North American.

Italy can be divided roughly into four areas. The North, the busiest area, goes from the west French boarder to Venice and Trieste east. This part of Italy comprises the major industrial and commercial resources:

Turin (Torino,in Italian), capital of Piedmont, and its metropolitan area have a population of 2.2 million. It is the seat of Fiat – Fabrica Italiana Automobile Torino – and often referred to as "the Automobile Capital of Italy" or the Detroit of Italy;

Milan (Milano) is the capital of Lombardy. The city proper has a population of about 1,318,000, while its metropolitan area has a 7.4 million population, expanded all over the central section of Lombardy region. Today Milan is a major centre for the production of textile and garments, automobile (Alfa Romeo and Pirelli tyres), chemicals, industrial tools, heavy machinery, book and music publishing. Its economic environment has made it, according to several studies, the world's 20th and Europe's 10th top business and financial centre. Originally a Celtic settlement, the city was conquered by the Romans in the 2d century BC. It suffered several invasions by the Visigoths, the Huns and the Ostrogoths in the 5th and 6th centuries, then by Longobards, who gave their name to the region. Milan surrendered to the Franks in 774 when Charlemagne took the title "King of the Lombards." Subsequently Milan was part of the Holy Roman Empire. Later Milan took part in the unceasing wars between Italian and other European states, and acquired the status of Duchy in 1183. In 1262, Ottone Visconti was created archbishop of Milan by Pope Urban IV, and opened the era of the House of the Visconti. Much of the prior history of Milan was the tale of the struggle between two political factions – the Guelphs and the Ghibellines. The Visconti family was able to seize power (*signoria*) in Milan, based on their "Ghibelline" friendship with the German Emperors. In 1395, Gian Galeazzo Visconti became duke of Milan. The Visconti family was to retain power in Milan for a century and a half from the early 14th century until the middle of the 15th century. In 1447, Filippo Maria Visconti, Duke of Milan, died without a male heir; following the end of the Visconti line, after a period of unrest, Milan was conquered by Francesco Sforza, of the

ITALY

House of Sforza, which made Milan one of the leading cities of the Italian Renaissance.

From the 15th until the 18th century, Milan was in the center of the fighting between French kings and the Habsburgs of Spain and Austria. The treaty of Utrecht formally confirmed Austrian sovereignty over most of Spain's Italian possessions including Lombardy and its capital, Milan.

In the 19th century, Milan was caught in the turmoil of Napoleonic wars, until the Congress of Vienna returned it to Austria in 1815. In 1848, the Milanese rebelled against Austrian rule and participated in the struggle for the Italian unification.

Monza, population 120,000, is internationally known for its motor racing circuit, home to the Italian Grand Prix. Situated 15 km northeast of Milan, it is an important economic, industrial, and administrative centre, supporting a textile industry and a publishing trade.

Parma, population 177,000, is one of Italy's most beautiful cities of art, cultural tourism, and gastronomic destination, known for its romantic monuments, castles, art, cuisine, and opera.

Parma is the native town to Giuseppe Verdi and Arturo Toscanini, Giovannino Guareschi (the author of Don Camillo), and to Bernardo Bertolucci (film director). This is the home of the University of Parma, one of the oldest universities in the world.

It is a city in the Italian region of Emilia-Romagna famous for its food and rich gastronomical tradition:

EUROPE DIGEST FOR THE HURRIED TOURIST

Parmigiano Reggiano cheese (also produced in Reggio Emilia), Prosciutto di Parma (Parma ham), and Balsamic vinegar.

Bologna is the capital city of Emilia-Romagna, in the Po Valley. The city lies between the Po River and the Apennine Mountains.

Home to the oldest university in the world, founded in 1088, Bologna is one of the most developed cities in Italy. Made 2,000's European Capital of Culture, it is lively and cosmopolitan, and has a rich history, art, cuisine, music and culture

In 2010, there were 375,944 people residing in Bologna (while 1 million live in the greater Bologna area).

A description of the city is given further in this book.

Padua, together with Venice, belongs to the Veneto region. Padua's population is 212,500. The city is sometimes included, with Venice, in the Padua-Venice Metropolitan Area, having a population of c. 1,600,000. Padua is located 40 km west of Venice and 29 km southeast of Vicenza. The Brenta River, which once ran through the city, still touches the northern area of the town and connects it with the Venice lagoon.

Description further down.

The center part of the Italian peninsula includes Florence, Pisa, and Rome.

The south is called Mezzogiorno by the Italians and is a difficult area. No industry, poor soil and a rough climate bring stagnant poverty; the north is continuously subsidizing this part of Italy. It starts in the region of Naples and

ITALY

goes down to Calabria.

Finally, Sicily can be considered as a separate region due to its climate, people, customs, and other particularities. Mezzogiorno and Sicily have always been the main sources of Italian emigration to the United States. Between 1820 and 1989, 5,360,000 Italians immigrated to America. Today, Italy faces the illegal immigration of thousands of Albanians and North Africans. From Italy, the immigrants can pass illegally to France and Germany, since Italy, France and Germany belong to the Schengen Space, which has no border control.

THE ITALIANS

The Italians are a collection of people. They think of themselves first as Romans, Milanese, Sicilian, or Florentines. Indeed, the regions of Italy are very different from one another; this regionalism is understandable, considering that Italy as a nation has only existed since 1866. Before this unification, the Italian peninsula was a conglomerate of independent states. Every now and then, Italians do make an effort to be nationalistic, for instance, when the Italian football team is doing well in the World Cup or when Ferrari wins a Grand Prix. And they definitely feel like Italians when they are expatriates. The typical stereotype describes Italians as a noisy, Mediterranean people, whose brilliance and inventiveness are unfortunately marred by laziness and unreliability. They are seen as a happy, fun-loving people with a genius for design, fashion, and food. They are also known to be wonderful at singing and at cooking. Italian men have black long hair, nine-inch hips, and are demon lovers. Italian women are incredibly attractive until they marry, when they become short, fat, and overweight mammas. Overseas-born Italians often imagine that Italy has not changed since their grandparents left it at the turn of the century. When they finally come to Italy to find their roots and visit their cousins, they are surprised to discover that not all families are poor, have ten children and live in one room which they share with a donkey, that not all the women wear black and work in the fields, nor that all men wear hats and sit in bars all day long. Italy is one of the world's most advanced countries, where most families have a least two cars and live in houses that not only have water and electricity but also televisions, videos, cell phones, and jacuzzis. The relationship between the children of the Italian immigrants and the country where they live is sometimes peculiar: if they are rich and successful, they will be regarded as Italian rather than as American or Australian. For instance, Frank Sinatra, Francis Ford Coppola, and Robert de Niro will always be considered as Italians.

How they see rich foreigners

Italians love foreigners, especially rich foreigners. The Austrians, Swiss, and Germans have always considered Italy as their playground. Ever since the days of the Roman Empire, the Italians have spent a lot of time getting rid of the foreign invaders, but these invasions are tolerated if the

ITALY

Italians get something in exchange. They are quite happy as long as the 20 million tourists that come to Italy every year spend lots of money, and return home.

How they see poor foreigners

Foreign immigration into Italy has been a problem since the late 1980s. More and more people arrive from Albania, Eastern Europe, Senegal, and the Maghreb. The Italian attitude towards the peoples of southern Europe and Northern Africa is a mixture of solidarity and disdain.

How they see themselves

The Italians see themselves a passionate and charming, and they like to act this part for the benefit of foreigners.

North and South

The Italian internal differences are often simplified into the difference between North and South. The Northern Italian views the Southerner as a corrupt, half-Arab peasant, who tolerates the Mafia and lives off the income generated by the hard-working North. The Southern Italian views the Northerner as a semi-literate, half-Austrian, half-French unwashed peasant who, by accident of birth, dwells in the richest part of the country and lives off the profit generated by the hard work produced by the Southerners. The differences in language, diet, and habits between the two areas are indeed large. The Southerners have a diet based on pasta and olive oil; the Northerners, on maize, rice, and butter. The language variations are so big that some movies produced in the South are dubbed for the North Italian market.

Italy is a country of contradictions.

It is the country of the Catholic Church, but also of the Mafia. It is the most pro-European country in Europe, but one of the worst at implementing EU directives. It is a country of enormous wealth and extreme poverty. Wealth and poverty live aside each other without giving the impression that the poor resent their wealthy neighbor's proximity. The only real social division is based on wealth. Those who have money show it and will be treated as VIPs, as long as they have enough, of course.

The Italians are great melodramatic actors. They learn how to act when they are children and go on acting throughout their lives. Being "on show" is their everyday behavior; the most important thing is to act and look the part. Their melodramatic character explains the popularity of operas in the 19th century. Today, it explains the incredible boom of karaoke, which gives them a wonderful opportunity to be on show in front of friends and family.

The most important thing is to have a fine figure (*bella figura*). Dressing well, taking life easy, and being seen to take things easy are part of bella figura. This is why Italians are so fond of proper dress: immaculate shirts, neatly pressed trousers, and suits in the latest fashion are very important, even for the poorer classes. They observe how other people dress, especially foreigners, who are generally considered to dress badly. The concept of outsmarting other Italians,

ITALY

who can then be mocked and laughed at, is essential and considered as a positive virtue. Slickness is even admired, so long as the guy gets away with it. Jumping in front of a traffic jam and roaring off at the light will be admired. If you are then stopped by the police, others will drive by with a contemptuous smile. If you get a ticket, well, it is still possible that you will never pay it...

Avoiding tax is one of the fields where Italians excel, and *economia sommersa* (hidden economy) is widely practiced. It has been estimated that one-third of Italy's economic activity is carried out unofficially. Italians are masters at *arrangiarsi* ("getting by"). Nothing seems to be impossible, and an arrangement is always found for any kind of situation. Consequently, patronage (*raccomandazione*), along with its trade of favors, jobs and influence, is part of Italian business life, especially when one knows of the incredible bureaucracy hindering any formality. It has been calculated that, to be entirely in line with the law, an Italian citizen should know some 800,000 rules. No wonder that hundreds of thousands of civil servants are kept in gainful employment, all of them demanding a most respectful attitude when you want to get somewhere without waiting for years.

The Italians are generous people, but their generosity is always tied to a system of return. If someone accepts a gift, he owes the giver a favor and virtually signs an agreement that can last a lifetime. If an Italian gives you a lift to the station, or the address of a good dentist, eventually he will expect something in return.

Punctuality is only relative in Italy, particularly in Rome. Lining up is an unknown principle: boarding a train looks like a busy afternoon at the stock exchange.

Soccer is the national sport, and the nation comes to a halt when the Italian team plays an important match. It is also the moment when Italians really feel like a nation – in front of their TV set.

Etiquette

The Italians are very courteous and well-mannered people. Hand-shaking and kissing are the norm. Strangers are addressed as *signore* (mister) and *signora* (madam). *Signorina* is used for unmarried young girls; if in doubt, signora is used. Professional titles are very often used, such as *professore* for professors and learned people, *dottore* for doctors or any graduates; *ingegnere*, *avvocato*, and *maestro* not only for musicians but also for any praised craftsman, etc. If the titles do not correspond exactly, it doesn't matter as long as they flatter the recipient.

When dining, alike on the entire European continent, one uses left and right hands together: the fork is held with the left hand, whilst the right hand uses the knife to cut meats, or push the food on the fork.

Entering a church requires proper dressing. No bare legs for men or arms for women are allowed, and women's heads should be covered. In main churches, a guard can prohibit the entrance to people not correctly dressed.

A decent dressing is also recommended when entering a classy restaurant, or attending a society party or diner.

ITALY

Shopping

Italians love shopping. It is considered as fun, especially at markets where bargains are to be found. Be careful, though, as a real bargain could prove to be a real fake. Bargaining is practiced on a large scale (see hereunder).

TV

Although the Italians didn't actually invent trash television, they have certainly brought it to a fine art. Innumerable broadcasting stations show films, cartoons and soap operas, all of them dubbed appallingly. Talk shows can go on for hours, and variety family shows all look alike. Of course, the candid camera is a favorite. The worst sitcoms take a certain spice when dubbed in Italian, and some completely unknown and second-rate actors have become stars in Italy.

Food

Italians are food centric. Whenever possible, meals are eaten in company. *Compania* derives actually from *con* ("with") and *pane* ("bread"). A typical meal may consist of *aperitivo*, – *antipasto*, (hors-d'oeuvre) – *pasta* (generic term designating an extraordinary palette of macaroni, spaghetti, cannelloni, lasagne, tagliatelli, farfelli, rigatoni, fusilli, etc. Italians eat an average of 28 kg each of pasta per year) – *secondo* (main dish) with *contorno* (sides) – *insalata* (salad) – *formaggio*, – *frutta* and/or dessert. A celebratory meal can take up to four hours. It finishes with the compulsory "*espresso*". The best espresso in Italy is said to be served in Bologna, one in which a spoon plunged should stand up straight.

EUROPE DIGEST FOR THE HURRIED TOURIST

American or English coffee will rarely be found in Italy, except in hotels frequented by foreigners. The nearest equivalent to an American coffee is the *caffè lungo*, espresso with hot water.

Some variations of espresso are *caffè macchiato* (with a few drops of cold or warm milk), *caffè lungo* (less concentrated than espresso), *caffè decaffeinato* (decaffeinated), *cappuccino* (espresso with steamed milk), *caffè latte* (mixture of caffè lungo and milk).

With food, a large assortment of wines is offered, of which the best known are:

- Chianti, a red wine produced in Tuscany. It is often associated with the famous round shaped bottle enclosed in a straw basket, although most of the producers use today classical botles;
- Valpolicella, light red wine from the Verona area;
- Soave, dry white wine, also from Verona;
- Lambrusco, light sparkling red wine from Lombardy;
- Asti Spumante, (sparkling white wine, generally sweet, from Piedmont;
- Frascati, dry white wine from the Roman Hills;
- Lacrima Christi, literally Christ's tears, a sweet white wine from the region of Naples;
- "Est!Est!!Est!!!." this peculiar name of a white wine from the region of Rome has a story. In 1111, a bishop named Fugger travelled from Germany to Rome. He sent his servant to taste the wines in the different inns where he was to stay. If the wines

ITALY

were good, the servant would leave a mark near the door: Est ("it is") if the wine was good or Non Est if it was not. Reaching the inn in Montefiascone, the servant was so enthusiastic about the wine that he wrote, Est! Est! Est! This wine is actually not a top brand, but is worth trying it for fun and the memory of Bishop Fugger.

Italy is also a great producer of mineral waters, which are widely consumed.

SEASONED TRAVELER'S TIPS

Hotels and restaurants

Although they may welcome you with great demonstrations of joy and love, waiters and receptionists do not expect any personal contact. Do not indulge in it. Do not joke with them. Italians love to laugh about tourists behind their back, or even openly, as you do not understand what they say about that funny shirt or your hairdo. A plain or grim face will encounter more respect than a cheerful, kindly one. Do not say "sorry" to the personnel, unless the waiter stumbles on your extended leg with a full tray of fish in creamy sauce or a similar situation. It is better to bother the servants with particular requests than to accept bluntly what they want you to order: this will prove you are a demanding client and you will consequently be treated better. When entering a restaurant, do not accept to sit at the first table shown if you don't like it. In classy restaurants, the custom wants you to let the maître d'hôtel make suggestions without asking the menu card. In that case, prices remain unknown, but, generally, there is no treachery. If what he offers is not to your taste, then asking for the menu is acceptable. Be careful: quite often meat and fish are priced *"per etto"*. It means the price is given per 100 g: ignoring this might lead to a bad surprise when the bill comes... Another peculiarity in Italy is that the garnish (*contorno*) is not included, and should be ordered separately. Until quite recently, there was a cover charge, but this is now disappearing.

Act as if you had been in the country 100 times. Ask about the wines, including own local wine and specialties. Talking about the menu brings you and the waiter, or the owner, in osmosis on a common interest: food.

Do not hesitate to change the menu. For instance, a pizza Napoletana has mozzarella cheese, tomatoes, anchovies, and olives. You may ask for capers to be added, or no anchovies, etc. Tipping is recommended (5 to 10%, if you are satisfied with the service). It is always better to under-tip (you will be considered a difficult customer) than to over-tip (you will be scorned as an untraveled peasant). Counting small change in front of the waiter is in poor taste: have the account ready, or pull out a big note. Check discretely, however, the change when it comes back. Today, handing over a credit card without a glance at the bill is ultimate class.

As a conclusion, these recommendations will not

guarantee 100 % that you will not be served yesterday's re-warmed dish, or a defrosted one, but you will in most cases receive better consideration than the lost and helpless average tourist will.

Shops

In all shops, after you have shown your desire to buy an item, ask if there is a discount. You might be surprised how many classy places will grant you something. In bazaars, open markets, and when sales are on, the basic approach to bargaining should be as follows:

First, don't show any interest for the item you want to buy. Among other articles, ask casually about "that one." With a bit of scorn, offer two-fifths of the price asked. The seller should then reduce it by a minimum of 10%. Your offer might increase to 50% of the price; the seller should allow another 10%, and so on until a price is fixed at mutual satisfaction. Remember, it is expected that you will bargain – this is part of the fun. If you pay without asking for anything, you will certainly lose all consideration.

Of course, you can't bargain on drinks in cafés, food in restaurants, or groceries, newspapers, bus tickets, etc. Department stores do not usually grant discounts, but you can always ask... If you feel that a discount could have been given to you but was bluntly refused, walk away. The sales clerk might run behind you to make you come back. If not, go to the next shop. If several shops nearby sell the same sort of merchandise, visit two or three to find the cheapest one or the one giving the biggest discount.

WHAT TO BUY IN ITALY

Fashion: Italy, mainly Rome, Milano, and Florence, has always been and continues to be the cradle of fashion creation and experimentation. Italian fashion designers are world famous, and sell around the planet: Giorgio Armani, Salvatore Ferragamo, Dolce & Gabbana, Gucci, Moschino, Prada, Emilio Pucci, Trussardi, Valentino, Versace, etc.

The difference in prices between designers' shops in Italy and their sub-companies in the European Union is almost inexistent. Only the non-European residents will still find an advantage because of the tax refund.

Except for the major shoemakers, such as Rossetti, Prada, Fendi, Gianfranco Ferré, Moschino, and Ferragamo, Italian shoes are often made for Southern European dry climates – which could mean many surprises when worn in pouring rain… Usually, even if the Italian shape and line are very "in", shoes made in Germany, England or Switzerland will give more use and satisfaction for an equivalent price – Clark's, Church's, or Winston in England, Bally in Switzerland.

Rome and Florence are the best places for leather belts, wallets, purses, and bags.

On the open markets, one mostly finds imitations, usually produced in North Africa or Asia. For snobbery or fun, you can buy one of those, but then apply the rules of bargaining. Be warned that you are doing this illegally, as it is forbidden to purchase or smuggle imitations. Avoid street-sellers of souvenirs such as little papier-mâché or musical

ITALY

boxes, glass-bead necklaces, sunglasses, etc. Department stores sell the same stuff at more reasonable prices.

All kinds of religious souvenirs, as well as others, can be found at Salviati in Rome. There are two huge Salviati shops on St. Peter's Square.

Venice is recommended for glass and crystal. You can easily have the famous Murano big candelabras shipped abroad. The best approach is to visit directly a manufacturer on the island of Murano. Some factories provide a free boat service (and don't forget the bargaining). Also in Venice, a nice souvenir is a carnival mask.

For collectors or children, Ferrari's small replicas are available everywhere.

EUROPE DIGEST FOR THE HURRIED TOURIST

ROME

Twenty seven centuries of history and art!! The 2,765th birthday of Rome will be celebrated on April 21, 2012.

Rome (Roma), is the capital of Italy and the country's largest and most populated city, with over 2.7 million residents. Rome's metropolitan area is also the largest in Italy with some 4.2 million residents. The city is located in the Lazio region. It extends over seven hills situated on both sides of the River Tiber. The seat of the Pope is at Vatican City, a sovereign state within Rome. The River Tiber divides the city. On the east bank are the most visible and plentiful remains of classical Rome. To the northwest and along the Tiber lies medieval Rome. Rome is famous for its many squares, fountains, statues, and palaces. The city has more than 12 sq miles of public gardens and parks. On the west bank of the Tiber are the Vatican City and the old quarter of Trastevere (literally "across Tiber"), which has maintained much of its medieval charm.

Rome is the financial, cultural, transportation, and administrative center of Italy. The banking, insurance, printing, publishing, and fashion industries are quite important. The thriving Italian movie industry is centered at Cinecitta (Cinema City), located a few miles outside of Rome, which is the largest movie town after Hollywood. Fourteen daily newspapers are published in Rome (the leading paper is the conservative Il Messaggero), and the two state-owned television channels and three radio channels are based there. The Vatican publishes its own newspaper, L'Osservatore

ITALY

Romano, and operates its own radio station, Radio Vatican. Rome is an important transportation center, with four major railway stations, including the main Termini station, and two international airports: Ciampino (an older airport, southeast of the city) and Leonardo da Vinci at Fiumicino (the newer facility, to the southwest). The city's subway system, Metropolitana, opened in 1952; it operates now two lines, with a third scheduled to open before 2015.

The economy of Rome depends heavily on tourism. Rome receives an average of 7–10 million tourists a year, which sometimes doubles on holy years. A record was broken in the 2000 Christian Jubilee Year with 32 million visitors.

Many of Rome's museums are among the world's greatest. The Vatican Museums and Galleries contain the richest collections. The city's ancient ruins include the Coliseum, the Catacombs, the Forum, the Arch of Constantine, the Baths of Caracalla, the Circus Maximus, the Capitol, and the Pantheon.

Rome has at least forty ancient catacombs, or underground burial places under or near the city, of which some were discovered only in recent decades. Though most famous for Christian burials, they include pagan and Jewish burials, either in separate catacombs or mixed.

Rome is well known for its many piazzas (squares), including the Piazza del Popolo, Piazza di Spagna, Piazza Colonna, Piazza Quirinale, and Piazza Navona. At the south end of Corso (the major street in Rome), a monument to Victor Emmanuel II commemorates the unification of Italy in the 19th century. Its architecture has led Romans to scornfully call it "the typewriter").

HISTORY OF ROME

Legend says that the history of Rome started around 1152 BC with the arrival of Eneus, who was fleeing with his family from Troy. He married Lavinia, the daughter of King Latinus. Their children founded the city of Alba, which is considered as the origin of Rome. In fact, many different people lived in Italy at that time, and the origin of Rome more accurately lies in Umbria, between Florence and Rome, with the settlement of Etruscans, who likely came from Illyria (present-day Croatia) or Greek islands around 900 BC and merged with the local people. Much of their very advanced art, religion, and rules were adopted by Roman civilization. Beginning around 775 BC, the southern part of Italy was being colonized by the Greeks, who brought with them their religion and culture, which also influenced Rome.

Settlements probably began about 1000 BC on Rome's future site in the surrounding hills, which unlike other low-lying areas of Latium were free of malaria. As the tradition says, two descendants of Eneus, Numitor and Amulius, went into conflict. Numitor abandoned his throne, and his daughter, Rhea Silvia, was condemned by Amulius to become a Vesta nun. She was so beautiful that the God Mars fell in love with her. She bore him two sons, Romulus and Remus. They were discovered by Amulius, who abandoned them in a basket on the river Tibre. Found and fed by a she-wolf (which became the symbol of Rome), they were cared for by a couple of shepherds. They discovered their origin as adults, overthrew Amulius, and put Numitor back on the throne.

They decided to create a city on the Palatino hill, right above the place where they were found by the she-wolf, on April 21, 735 BC. The legend says that Romulus ploughed a large circular furrow and proclaimed loudly, "Any one penetrating this boundary will be put to death!" Remus, hearing this, jokingly stepped over the line, and Romulus slew his own brother on the spot. According to the relation made by Livy in "History of Rome," Remus was in fact killed in a fight about who should be king of the new city. Romulus made his town an asylum for fugitives from other countries, outlaws, but these were only men, and there were no women to create families. They planned an assault on the nearby city of Sabia and kidnapped all of the women, which led to war. At the end of this war, Rome and Sabia merged. Romulus ruled as the first King of Rome from 753 - 715 BC. He was known as a warrior king who developed Rome's first army while expanding Rome's territory. Meanwhile, the Etruscan kingdom developed; in the 6th century BC, it gave three kings to Rome. The third one, Tarquinius Superbus, (Tarquin the Proud) ruled from 534-510 BC. Under his rule, the Etruscans were at the height of their power, and the authority of the monarchy was absolute. He repealed several earlier constitutional reforms and used violence and murder to hold his power. The Romans despised his tyrannical rule, and revolted in 510 BC. The Tarquins and the monarchy were cast out of Rome. The Senate voted to never again allow the rule of a king, and a republican government was formed. This regime would last until the fall of the Roman Empire in 509 AD (even the later imperial government maintained forms of the republican system). Free from the rule of kings, the Romans developed a strict social status hierarchy that would set in motion the conquest of the Western World. Vanquished and annexed by Rome, the Etruscans continued to have their own customs and culture until the end of the 3rd century BC

The early city was built on seven hills. Capitoline Hill and Palatine Hill (nearest the east bank of the Tiber) were the first sites of the city; between them was the Roman Forum. The city eventually became the capital of the Roman Empire. During the 5th century AD, the city entered a period of decline and was sacked by the Visigoths under Alaric I and by the Vandals. Temporal political and social authority in the city of Rome was gradually gathered in the hands of the bishop of Rome, later named the Pope, who began to claim primacy among western bishops. In 754, the Popes, with Frankish aid, were able to assert their independence and hegemony over a large portion of central Italy called the Papal States, with Rome as their capital. Nevertheless, Rome suffered a severe decline during the Middle Ages. The city became the scene of power struggles between Rome's leading families, especially the Orsini and Colonna, the Papacy, and secular rulers. Factional struggles such as that between the Guelphs and Ghibellines con-

ITALY

tinued during the 13th century. When the Papacy moved to Avignon, France, during the 14th century, Rome experienced one of its most serious declines. Rome began its great recovery under Papal guidance during the second half of the 15th century. By the mid-16th century, the city saw numerous new and splendid buildings constructed and ancient monuments rebuilt, as art and architecture enjoyed a renaissance. Growth continued in the later 16th century as population steadily increased, and Rome again became a premier world city. In 1870, when the Papal States joined the newly created Kingdom of Italy, Rome, the capital, had a population exceeding 225,000 inhabitants. In 1929, the Lateran Treaty created the separate state of Vatican City within the city, and, being the Papal city, Rome escaped damage during WWII.

THE ROMAN LEGION

The Roman Army has been invincible for almost eight centuries and has conquered a territory covering southern and central Europe, England, the near East, and North Africa. The Army is composed of legions (the equivalent to modern divisions), each of them 6,000 to 8,000 men strong. It splits into 10 cohorts, each one subdivided into three maniples, consisting of two centuries. All these units can maneuver by themselves and are highly mobile.

The legion comprises:
- Heavy infantry (Hoplites), who carry about 55 pounds of equipment including helmet, breast-

plate, a large square shield, a long spear, a javelin, a sword, various tools and utensils for cooking, and cereals for 15 to 20 days;
- Light infantry (Velites), who carry much less and are very mobile;
- Cavalry, who conduct reconnaissance, and conduct attacks from the rear and on the sides;
- Archers;
- An engineering corps, which builds the camps, and is responsible for the various heavy equipment, including catapults and siege machines.

The Centuries are Companies of 80 to 100 men, commanded by a Centurion (Major). The Decuries are platoons of 10 men, lead by Decurions. The infantry advances on three lines, with cavalry and mercenary troops on the sides. When fighting against the barbaric hordes, soldiers used to shave their heads to avoid being seized by the hair.

Around 200 BC, there were 28 legions; 200 years later, they were 33. In the first century, the Army included, with the mercenary and allied troops, approximately 1 million men. The commander in chief is the Consul, responsible to the Senate. Military service is compulsory, but the Army is also professional and open to all: the juniors, aged 17 to 46, serve on the field; the seniors, aged 46 to 60, serve in the towns in a corps equivalent to the US National Guard. The discipline is terrible, but the soldiers are well paid and well considered. They can receive a lot of rewards and ad-

ITALY

vantages. They represent a force which many ambitious Consuls have used to impress the Senate and the people and to acquire glory and power: Marius, Sylla, Pompeus, Cesar used the Army to gain dictatorship. After Nero's death, the Occident and Oriental Armies fought for the designation of their leader. The Oriental Army prevailed and imposed the Senate to elect their Chief Vespasianus to the imperial throne.

SISTINE CHAPEL

The Sistine Chapel is the private, official Papal Chapel where conclaves for the election of Popes are traditionally held. Its name comes from its commissioner, the Pope Sixtus IV who reigned from 1471 to 1485.

Built from 1473 to 1481, the Sistine Chapel is a rectangular brick building with six arched windows on each of the two main (or side) walls and a barrel-vaulted ceiling. It is 134 ft wide and 45 ft high. These dimensions correspond exactly to the dimensions of the Temple of Salomon in Jerusalem, as given by the Bible.

Visiting the Chapel

During the tourist season, huge lines form at the entrance, with a waiting time of two or three hours. If you travel on your own, it is strongly recommended to buy a ticket in advance or to join a guided private tour in order to skip the line.

To pre-order an entrance ticket: bigliatteriamusei.vatican.va

EUROPE DIGEST FOR THE HURRIED TOURIST

To join a guided tour: myvaticantour.com, or rome-tickets.com

Guides are not allowed to deliver commentary inside the Chapel. Therefore, the following description might be useful.

Between 1481 and 1483, Sixtus IV commissioned numerous artists to produce 14 fresco decorations illustrating the lives of Moses and Christ along the walls.

The official entrance to the chapel is on the east side, but the tour circuit takes visitors through an entrance situated on the opposite side (under the Last Judgment).

When entering the chapel: On the north wall (left-hand side) are six frescoes depicting events from the life of Christ painted by Perugino, Pinturicchio, Sandro Boticelli, Domenico Ghirlandaio, Cosimo Rosselli and Piero di Cosimo.

On the south wall (right-hand side) are six frescoes depicting events from the life of Moses, painted by Perugino, Botticelli, Cosimo Rosselli and Luca Signorelli.

Above these works, smaller frescoes between the windows depict various popes.

Between 1508 and 1512, the Pope Julius II commissioned Michelangelo to redecorate the barrel-vaulted ceiling. The Pope's original request was to paint the figures of the twelve apostles. Michelangelo found this a rather poor subject. The Pope agreed finally to give him carte blanche, and Michelangelo chose to decorate the 520 sq m ceiling with frescoes illustrating the Book of Genesis, from the Creation to the Flood. During the work,

ITALY

the ceiling could not be seen from down below because of the scaffolding. The Pope came almost every day asking Michelangelo when he would finish. He answered, "When I can." Finally, on the August 14, 1511, Julius II was allowed to see Michelangelo's work for the first time. One year later, the entire masterpiece was completed.

The triangles over the windows depict Christ's ancestors; between these triangles, figures of prophets and sibyls sit in illusionistic architectural niches surrounding the scenes.

In the corners of the ceiling, four scenes represent the heroes of the People of Israel (from right to left): Haman, David and Goliath, Judith and Holopherne, and the bronze snake.

In the center of the ceiling lies the famous Creation of the Universe and other scenes from the Old Testament. Facing from the entrance side, you will see the following panels:

- Panel 1: God separates light and darkness
- Panel 2: Creation of the sun, moon, and vegetation
- Panel 3: God separates earth from water and creates life in the sea
- Panel 4: Creation of Adam
- Panel 5: Creation of Eve
- Panel 6: Sin and expulsion from Paradise
- Panel 7: Noah's sacrifice
- Panel 8: The Flood
- Panel 9: Noah's drunkenness

Twenty years later, at the age of 60, Michelangelo was commissioned again by Popes Clement VII and Paul III to paint "The Last Judgment" on the wall above the altar (by the entrance).

The angels in the middle blow their horns to raise the dead. One of them holds the Book in which all has been written down and upon which Jesus will base his judgment.

To the left, the chosen are escorted to Heaven by angels.

To the right, the damned are going to Hell. Michelangelo was inspired by Dante's Inferno. Charon (with oar) and his devils are leading the damned to judge Minos (with snake).

In the center, Christ judges, and the Virgin Mary is near Him. The two large figures are Paul (left) and Peter (right, with keys in hand). The figure underneath and to the right of Jesus is St. Bartholomew - a self-portrait by Michelangelo. At the right bottom, Minos, the Judge of Hell, girded by a snake, is pictured by Michelangelo as the portrait of Biagio de Cesena, a pontifical officer who complained to the Pope about painting so many nudes in such a sanctified place.

Over the years, dirt and layers of varnish and glue applied at various times obscured the frescoes. In the 1980s, the Michelangelo paintings were cleaned to reveal their original colors, despite protests from some art lovers who feared that cleaning would damage them.

WHAT TO DO IN ROME

Before going to Rome, see one or several films:

"Quo Vadis" (1951), starring Robert Taylor, Deborah

ITALY

Kerr and Sophia Loren - "Roman Holiday" (1953), starring Audrey Hepburn and Gregory Peck - "Julius Cesar" (1953), starring Marlon Brando - "Ben Hur" (1959), starring Charlton Heston - "Spartacus" 1960, starring Kirk Douglas - "La Dolce Vita" (1960).

After having visited, preferably with a guided tour, the Roman Forum, the Coliseum, the Vatican, and Saint Peters Basilica, take a stroll in the heart of the city. Start with a cappuccino on one of the terraces in Campo dei Fiori, (Field of the flowers), which is perhaps the loveliest square in the old city. Every morning, there is a colorful flower, fruit, and vegetable market. In the evening, the Piazza is invaded by the Roman youth. From there, stroll north along the narrow streets to Piazza Navona. Built on the former Domitian stadium, and keeping the arena's oblong shape, this is a lively meeting place, with its three fountains, amongst which the Fountain of the Four Rivers, by Bernini. It was constructed between 1647 and 1651 on request of the Pope Innocent X. The fountain features four figures, each representing a river from a different continent – the Nile, Ganges, Danube and Rio della Plata.

Let us mention here the extraordinary devotion citizens of Rome have always given to water.

The nine aqueducts built by the successive Roman emperors gathered large amounts of water from the Latin hills, and permitted to supply not only Imperial household, private villas and thermal public baths, but also 591 public basins, and 39 monumental fountains, which exist today.

From Piazza Navona, east to the Pantheon, a temple

beautifully preserved, built by Agrippa in 27 BC. The antique dome covering the inside is, even nowadays, an architectural wonder. The chapels contain the tombs of the Italian kings as well as that of the painter Raphael.

Further east, crossing the main artery of Rome, the Via del Corso, one comes to the Fountain of Trevi, made famous by the Fellini movie la Dolce Vita, with sumptuous Anita Ekberg taking a bath in it.

A traditional legend holds that if visitors throw two coins into the fountain, they are ensured a return to Rome. This should be done with one's right hand over one's left shoulder. An estimated 3,000 Euros are thrown into the fountain each day. The money has been used to subsidize a supermarket for Rome's needy.

Then finish with, to the north, Piazza di Spagna, with its majestic Spanish Steps.

If not too tired, go shopping at the adjacent Via dei Condotti, where you will meet the most fashionable Roman women shopping at Valentino, Armani, or Max Mara. An alternative is to visit the Trastevere (Trans-Tiber), on the west-bank of the Tiber. This is the oldest part of Rome, and a favorite area to Romans, with its small streets, shops, trattorias, wine bars, and an incredible flea market at the Porta Portese, where anything and everything can be found, including the watch or the bag stolen from you the day before. After the fall of the Roman Empire, an important Jewish community was once based in Trastevere, later transferred to the Jewish ghetto on the east-side od the Tiber. There lies also the major synagogue in Rome, the Tempio Maggiore.

EATING PLACES

There are many thousands of restaurants, including hundreds of Pizzerias, all around Rome. It is difficult to make a survey.

When stopping at an unknown random place, peruse the menu hanging outside and look for crowded tables.

There is a certain hierarchy in the standing of the restaurants:

Pizzerias specialise in pizza and can range from a tiny bar counter to a luxurious establishment. In Italy, pizza tends to be a bargain: a personal-size pizza is always cheaper than a multicourse meal. It's filling, unlikely to be disappointing, and usually arrives at your table fairly quickly, which makes pizza especially attractive after a long day of sightseeing.

Osterias (sometimes Hostaria) are former inns or taverns. They serve homestyle food at generally moderate prices and may have a picturesque decor and top-level dining.

Trattorias are family-run restaurants with home-cooking and cozy atmospheres. They may also be renowned and snobbish with relevant prices.

Rosticcerias specialize in roasted or barbecued meat, which means a tendency for more sophisticated service and prices.

The name *ristorante* covers all other types of restaurants. Here are five of my favorites:

EUROPE DIGEST FOR THE HURRIED TOURIST

Osteria Da Meo Patacca
Piazza dei Mercanti. 065 806187 (Trastevere)

Da Meo Patacca is a restaurant, a nightclub, and a carefree beer parlor. It is housed in an ancient stable in the heart of Trastevere and sprawls the entire piazza De' Mercanti, glittering with lanterns hung from the stately old trees that provide an enormous umbrella for the entire square.

It was opened by Remington Olmsted, former U.C.C.L.A. football star, dancer and student of opera, who married an Italian girl, Diana, daughter of Daniele Varè, former ambassador and author of "The Laughing Diplomat."

For evening dinner, this is a huge and lively place, with troubadours who sing everything from naughty Trastevere songs and romantic melodies of Naples to grand opera and American songs. There is even an equestrian show. Fantastic!

Prices moderate: Main courses 12 – 20€. House wine 10€.

Da Pancrazio
Piazza del Biscione 92. Tel. 066 861246 (Historical center near Campo dei Fiori)

Adiacent to the Piazza di Campo de' Fiori, Da Pancrazio is built on the ruins of Pompeus' antique Theatre that has been transformed into one of the most original buildings in Italy. The restaurant room upstairs is 19th century, but in the restaurant downstairs, one can dine within the ruins of one of the most magnificent buildings in ancient Rome, which at that time could accomodate 28,000 spectators.

Prices are moderate. Reservations are recommended.

ITALY

Osteria Picchioni
Via del Boschetto 16. Tel. 06 4885261;

Situated in the center of Rome, near the National Gallery of Modern Art and the Bank of Italy and frequented by Italian politicians, this is the kingdom of Pizza – with a capital P. The huge oven is used to cook gigantic pizzas. Not much atmosphere, and neon lighting, but the amount of food, the quality, and the prices are really worth it.

Alfredo alla Scrofa
Via della Scrofa 104 (Near Piazza Navona and the Pantheon)

Tel 06-68806163 Metro: Spagna

A mythical place for Americans.

Alfredo, the "King of the Fettuccine," launched his restaurant in 1907. A few years later, he created the famous Fettuccine Alfredo, which became famous thanks to Mary Pickford and Douglas Fairbanks, who tried this plate in the restaurant on Via della Scrofa during their honeymoon and brought it back to Hollywood. Since then, scores of movie stars have patronized the establishment and left their photographs, which cover the walls. Main courses are priced from €15 to 24. Reservations recommended.

Ristorante Aroma at Palazzo Manfredi
Via Labicana, 125 – 00184 Rome
Website: hotelgladiatori.it/ita/la_terrazza.htm
Tel. +39 06 77591380

Palazzo Manfredi resides above the original gladiator

EUROPE DIGEST FOR THE HURRIED TOURIST

training grounds of Imperial Rome. Magnificently set in open air on the roof terrace of Palazzo Manfredi, the restaurant offers a fantastic view, with the Coliseum and the Imperial Forum literally surrounding you. Prices are high, but this is a magical experience, best in the evening when, after sunset, the monuments are floodlighted.

TUSCANY

Tuscany is one of the most appealing areas in Italy. Its scenery has inspired many painters of the Renaissance period, with its small hills, cypress and olive trees, terraced gardens, and Renaissance villas. The blue of the sky seems to have a particular gentleness. Tuscany also has a seacoast with resorts such as Viareggio, where Puccini composed La Bohême, Madame Butterfly, and La Tosca. Further out lies the island of Elba, where Napoleon was deported in 1814, and from where he escaped in 1815 for his return to France. Florence is the major town, but other cities are famous, such as Sienna, which gave its name to the color "burnt sienna," and Pisa, renowned for its leaning tower.. Tuscany is the place where Italian cuisine was born, at the court of the Medici. Florence has many specialties such as the Bistecca alla Fiorentina (thick steak) or Bistecca alla costata (T-bone steak), cod dressed in olive oil and garlic, white or red beans in olive oil with garlic and onions, and, of course, the famous Chianti wines.

FLORENCE

Population: 400,000

Florence (Firenze) needs no introduction as the birthplace of the Italian Renaissance. It is the capital of the arts and of the Italian genius. For more than 300 years, it has been the cradle of an exceptional artistic output. Nowhere else are to be found such a large number of magnificent

EUROPE DIGEST FOR THE HURRIED TOURIST

Renaissance works of architecture, sculpture, and painting. It would take days to see everything, from the beautiful cathedral and its baptistery, Palazzo Vecchio (City Hall) and Piazza della Signoria, Ponte Vecchio (The Old Bridge), Medici and Pitti Palaces, to the Galleria degli Uffizi, one of the world's leading art gallery.

Florence has given birth to some of the Humanity's greatest genius in the fields of art, literature, and architecture.

Painting and sculpture

In Italian history of Art, the century is usually named by the hundreds: *duecento* = 1200 or 13th century, *trecento* = 1300 or 14th century, *quatrocento* = 1400 or 15th century, and so on),

- Duecento (13th century): Cimabue – Giotto
- Trecento (14th century(: Andrea da Firenze – Lorenzo Monaco – Donatello
- Quatrocento/Cinquecento (15th/16th century): Fra Angelico – Fra Bartolomeo – Sandro Boticelli – Andrea de Castagno – Domenico Ghirlandaio – Filippo Lippi – Tommaso Masaccio – Michelangelo – Perugino – Antonio Pollaiolo – Raphael – Andrea del Sarto – Paolo Uccello – Domenico Veneziano – Leonardo da Vinci – Benvenuto Cellini

Architecture

Leon Battista Alberti – Brunelleschi – Pisano – Donatello – Lorenzo Ghiberti – Andrea Orcagna – Andrea della Robbia

ITALY

Literature
Dante Allighieri – Giovanni Boccaccio – Francesco Petrarch – Niccolo Machiavelli – Giorgio Vasari – Pietro Aretino

HISTORY

Florence was founded by Julius Caesar but became prosperous only in the 12th century, thanks to its merchants and bankers. These prosperous figures of Florentine economy founded dynasties and built themselves magnificent mansions and palaces. They also protected and sponsored many artists, attracting a lot of them to their court. During the 13th century, the wool and silk industry employed one-third of the population, and artisans, financed by Florentine bankers, exported their products all over Europe. Florence was an independent republic with a democratic government. The citizens were organized in corporations or guilds according to their profession. The guilds elected, for a period of two months, the Signoria, a chamber of nine Lords (Priori) that was endowed with important legislative and executive power. There was a fierce competition amongst eligible candidates. Rich bankers rivaled to impose their own men. The Strozzi, Medici, Pitti, Rucelli, Spini-Ferroni, and the Pazzi, who were lending money to the greatest kings in Europe, spent fortunes to get control of the Signoria.

This is how, the head of one of the most important bank in Florence – and in Europe –, Giovanni di Bicci of the Medici family, was elected as prime Lord in 1360. The Medici dynasty was to rule over Florence for twelve gen-

EUROPE DIGEST FOR THE HURRIED TOURIST

erations, giving four Popes to the Catholic Church and two queens to France (Catherine of Medici, who married Henri the second, and Mary of Medici, who married Henry IV).

Cosimo the Elder, Bicci's son, proved an extraordinary businessperson and politician. He ruled the city for 30 years. He was also a major patron of arts, and attracted to his circle the very best of Florentine intellectuals and artists, such as Brunelleschi, Donatello Paolo Uccello, Filippo Lippi, Fra Angelico and many others.

His grandson, Lorenzo the Magnificent (1449-1492), was the most famous of all the Medici for his princely ruling, his skilful diplomacy, and his enormous artistic and humanistic sensitivity. On the other hand, he did not prove able at managing the commercial and banking empire of the Medici; this led gradually to the decline of the financial power of the Dynasty.

There was an almost perpetual state of war between the various kingdoms, principalities, and autonomous states of Europe between the 13th and the 16th centuries. The marriages between the noble families of Italy used to bring fighting amongst the sons or successors, who tried to increase their power by concluding alliances with whichever state possible: Rome and the Pope, Venice, Milan, Naples, Spain, France, and German states. Florence, very much solicited for its financial power, kept hesitating between its alliance with the German Emperor, supported by the party of the Ghibellines, and the Pope, supported by the party of the Guelphs. Both the Emperor and the Pope, engaging in costly wars with France, Milano, Venice, and other states,

ITALY

searched for the support of wealthy Florence. As merchants and bankers were constantly fighting for power in the city, art and culture continued to flourish, sometimes mixed with violence, murders, and bloodshed. Benvenuto Cellini, for instance, jeweler, painter, musician, and writer of great talent and fame was also a hooligan involved in mysterious affairs of poisoning and stabbing. Being a master in fencing was a necessity, and strolling at night in the narrow streets was dangerous. Florence has been described as a vampire city: the rulers were merciless, and an innumerable number of people, accused of defying the ruling families, were executed publicly on the square in front of the Palazzo Vecchio: Francesco di Pozzi, who dared oppose the Medici, was scorched alive and left hanging on the facade wall of the palace. The monk Savonarole, who criticized the rulers' megalomania and dissoluteness, was burned alive in Piazza Della Signori. Leonardo da Vinci was always present at these executions to sketch the tortured people. In 1348, the plague decimated half of the population, and ended the struggle amongst the different factions. The Medici dynasty emerged as the final winner and ruled Florence until the 18th century.

GUELPHS AND GHIBELLINES

The names "Guelph" and "Ghibelline" came into use in Florence at the beginning of the 13th century. They were derived from the names of two great German families who disputed the throne of the Holy Roman Emperor in the 12th century. The Ghibellines were the supporters of the Lords of Waiblingen, the castle and the cradle of the Hohenstaufen Dynasty from Swabia. The Guelphs, members of the Welf Dynasty from Bavaria, were supporters of the Pope.

In the early 13th century, the Welfs, or Guelphs, allied with the Papacy in its struggle against the Hohenstaufen Emperor Frederick II for control of Italy. In general, the Guelphs drew their Italian support from the merchant class of the central italian communes, including Florence, and the French Dukes of Anjou, then rulers of Naples. The Ghibellines, gathering the imperial vicars of northern Italian cities, the communes of Siena and Pisa in Tuscany, and the feudal magnates of central Italy, attempted to regain control of the peninsula after Frederick's death in 1250. The Angevins of Naples and the Florentine Guelphs defeated them in 1268. Later, the names applied mainly to local factions or even families. Around 1300, membership in the Guelph party became a prerequisite for holding political office in Florence; thus, Guelfism was elevated to the status of a political ideology.

With the return of the Papacy from Avignon to Italy, and the creation of regional autonomous states in the 15th century, the terms dropped from use.

WHAT TO DO AND SEE IN FLORENCE

Florence is a city where every street corner can make the visitor discover an unexpected heartbreaking sight. When you emerge from a narrow shady street to find yourself abruptly confronted with the splendid multi-colored façade of the Cathedral, I challenge anyone who had this experience to say that he did not receive a shock.

If rushed by time, four exceptional sites are definitely not to be missed:

The Cathedral Santa Maria dei Fori

Santa Maria Dei Fiori (Saint Mary of The Flowers, also called The Duomo) is known for its distinctive Renaissance dome, engineered by Filippo Brunelleschi. The awesome impression given by the cathedral comes from the façade, covered with polychrome marble panels in various shades of green and pink bordered by white.

The Duomo dominates the skyline of Florence and is visible from far away.

It was the first octagonal cupola in history to be built without a wooden supporting frame, and was the largest hemispherical roof built at the time. It is still the largest masonry dome in the world.

The Ponte Vecchio (Old Bridge)

The oldest bridge in Florence, and the most famous, replaced a wooden bridge that had crossed the Arno River since Roman times. It is lined on both sides with shops. Originally, these were grocers, butchers, and fishmongers; by the end of the 15th century, perhaps because of their bad smell, the shops were assigned to goldsmiths and silversmiths. An opening midway across the bridge offers views of the river and shore. The upper side of the bridge, known as the Vasariano corridor, was designed by Vasari to link the Palazzo Vecchio and the Uffizi Gallery to the Pitti Palace. Today, it is an art gallery.

The Piazza della Signoria

When the medieval Guelf party finally prevailed over the Ghibellines, they razed part of the old city center to build a new palace for civic government, now called Palazzo Vecchio (Old Palace). The space around the Palazzo became the new civic center of town, with the L-shaped Piazza della Signoria, named after the oligarchic ruling body of the medieval city.

Today, it is an outdoor sculpture gallery, teeming with tourists, postcard stands, horses and buggies, and outdoor cafes. The statuary on the piazza is particularly beautiful, starting on the far left (as you are facing the Palazzo Vecchio) with Giambologna's equestrian statue of Grand Duke Cosimo I (1594). To its right is the Fontana del Nettuno (Neptune Fountain), created by Bartolomeo Ammannati as a tribute to Cosimo I's naval ambitions. The Florentines seem to hate it and nicknamed the statue Il Biancone ("Big Whitey").

On the other corner of the Palace stands Michelangelo's "David," a 19th-century copy of the original that is now in the Accademia Museum. Near enough to David to look truly ugly in comparison is Bandinelli's Heracles (1534). Poor Bandinelli tried to copy Michelangelo's muscular male form, but ended up making his Heracles merely lumpy.

At the piazza's south end is one of the square's ear-

ITALY

liest and prettiest embellishments, the Loggia dei Lanzi, named after the Swiss guard of lancers Cosimo de' Medici stationed here.

The Uffizi Gallery

Uffizi Gallery is one of the most famous museums of paintings and sculpture in the world. Its collection of primitive and Renaissance paintings comprises several universally acclaimed masterpieces of all time, including works by Giotto, Simone Martini, Piero della Francesca, Fra Angelico, Filippo Lippi, Botticelli, Mantegna, Correggio, Leonardo da Vinci, Raphael, Michelangelo and Caravaggio. German, Dutch, and Flemish masters are also well represented, with important works by Dürer, Rembrandt, and Rubens.

The Uffizi Gallery occupies the top floor of the large building erected by Giorgio Vasari between 1560 and 1580 to house the administrative offices of the Tuscan State.

In 1993, a car bomb exploded in adjacent Via dei Georgofili and damaged parts of the palace, killing five people. The identity of the bomber or bombers has never been established, although some suspect the Mafia.

The renovation took five years and cost $15 million. It added more than 20,000 square feet of new museum space, so allowing displaying more than 100 works that had never been seen before.

Today, the Uffizi is one of the most popular tourist attractions of Florence. In high season (particularly in July), waiting times can be up to five hours. You can avoid waiting by ordering a ticket in advance at www.uffizi-gallery.museum-ticket.it. This is also valid for the other museums in Florence.

Michelangelo's David

Accademia Museum

The Accademia delle Arti del Disegno – Arts of Drawing Academy – was founded in 1563 by Cosimo I de' Medici

The Gallery of the Accademia houses the original David by Michelangelo since 1873. The sculpture was brought from its previous outdoor location on Piazza della Signoria to the Accademia for reasons of conservation.

Viewed as a gallery piece, David looks odd; his upper body and head are both out of proportion. It is argued that the scale was deliberate, as from the original viewpoint of the viewer, the upper body would have been much farther away. This does not however explain the fact that the size of the hands is not in proportion with the rest of the body. Another amusing detail is that David has been given a squint by his creator, as discovered and exposed in detailed computerized images by Marc Levoy of Stanford University in Cal.

WHERE TO EAT

Cibreo

Via de Macci 118

Tel. 055 234 11 00

Authentic Tuscan food and excellent multi-language service. Without a reservation, there might be some waiting. Prices rather high.

The Cibreino, nearby, offers a shorter menu-card at cheaper prices (but no reservations).

L'Acquacotta
Via dei Pilastri 51.
Tel. 055 24 2907

A little bit off the city center, a block away from the Accademia Museum, this is a very small family-run restaurant, frequented by local customers as well as tourist. Excellent food at reasonable prices.

PISA

Pisa lay by the sea until the 15th century, by which time accumulated silt deposited by the Arno River had completely cut the city off from the receding shoreline. Ancient Pisa, or Pisae, was inhabited by the Ligurians before passing under Roman control as a naval base. It became a Roman colony shortly after 180 BC; by AD 313, it had become a Christian bishopric. Pisa survived the collapse of the Roman Empire to remain the principal urban center of Tuscany. With the help of Genoa, it also took the initiative against Muslim raiders. In 1016, the Pisans and Genoese drove the Saracens from Sardinia; in 1063, the Pisan fleet sacked Muslim Palermo. The city's participation in the

EUROPE DIGEST FOR THE HURRIED TOURIST

Crusades secured valuable commercial positions for Pisan traders in Syria; thereafter, Pisa grew in strength to rival Genoa and Venice. In the 13th century, Pisa, a Ghibelline city, enjoyed the support of German emperors in its long conflicts with Genoa at sea and with its Tuscan rivals, Lucca and Florence, on land. These struggles culminated in Pisa's defeat by the Genoese fleet at the decisive Battle of Meloria in 1284. Despite this defeat, Pisa remained the chief port of Tuscany. Internal factional struggles helped to bring about the occupation of Pisa by the Florentines in 1406.

The University of Pisa, founded in 1343, had more than 25,000 students in the late 20th century. Pisa was the birthplace of the scientist Galileo Galilei.

THE LEANING TOWER

The bell tower, begun in 1174 as the third and final structure of the city's cathedral complex, was designed to stand 185 feet (56 m) high and is constructed of white marble. Three of its eight levels were completed when the uneven settling of the building's foundation in the soft ground became noticeable. Bonanno Pisano, the engineer in charge, sought to compensate the leaning by making the new levels slightly taller on the short side, but the extra masonry caused the structure to sink even further. Work was suspended several times as engineers sought solutions, but the tower was still leaning when it ultimately topped out in the 14th century. Since the 11th century more than 8,000 projects have been presented to resolve the problem. As the tower was taking a leaning angle of a one-fifth of an inch per year, it was no longer possible to guarantee the safety of some 800,000 visitors/year. It was closed to the public on the January 7, 1987, for the first time since its construction in the 11th century. According to the mayor, closing was only planned for 3 months, but it took another 5 years of study before the work could be started in 1992. The first two levels were circled with steel cables gained with Teflon, and then 700 tons of lead were hung on the north side in an attempt to pull back and stabilize the cylinder. Once straightened, the tower then received a concrete base anchored in place by cables, 150 ft underground. The tower started leveling itself; the last stage, the casting of the concrete platform had begun when something unexpected was discovered at the bottom of the tower in 1995. It took some time before it was discovered that previous work had been done in 1934, and apparently not recorded. In the meantime, the tower sunk again. Architect-engineer Pierro Pierotti says that the work done was a mistake: the sinking side of the tower was compressing the ground, leading to a natural stabilization. By pulling the tower side backwards, one had created a hole in the underground. Today, 100 more tons of lead have stopped the sinking, but for how long? The chief of the building commission has recognized that a certain risk had been taken, but if nothing had been done, the tower would have collapsed within the next 200 years. To this day, $13 million of the initial $17 million budget have already been spent.

EUROPE DIGEST FOR THE HURRIED TOURIST

SIENA

Siena, the capital city of the Siena province in the Tuscany region, is situated about 55 km (35 miles) south of Florence in the heart of a region. It is known for its marble quarries and Chianti wine as well as the clay-earth pigment that gave the name to the color "burnt sienna." Siena has a population of 66,000. The town has largely retained the appearance of a large, prosperous medieval city, and for this reason is a popular tourist center. Many medieval and Renaissance palaces survive. The University of Siena dates back to the 13th century. Founded by Etruscans and later ruled by Rome and the Lombards, Siena became a free commune in the 12th century. In the 13th century, it became a flourishing banking center rivaling Florence. It was stricken by the Black Plague in 1348, when one-third of the population died. Emperor Charles V of Spain halted Siena's four centuries of republican autonomy in 1555, but Sienese rebelled and asked for France's King Henri II protection. The French siege lasted for more than a year.

In 1569, the city came under the rule of Medici Dukes of Tuscany. Siena thereafter shared the history of Tuscany, joining united Italy in 1860.

Catherine of Siena (1347-1380) was an Italian mystic. She joined the Dominican Order and is especially remembered for the part she played in bringing about the return of Pope Gregory XI from the papal residence in Avignon, France, to Rome. Convinced of the need to end the 68-year absence of the popes from Rome, Catherine traveled to

ITALY

Avignon to present her case personally and persuaded the pope to leave France in 1377. Siena is famous for its annual Palio delle Contrade, which takes place twice a year on the Piazza del Campo, one of the most beautiful squares in the world. The contrade (town-district parishes) prepare for this race year-round. After days of parading, the bareback horse race takes place around the square. It sometimes degenerates in a bloody fight, purging the animosity of the people against each other.

CONDOTTIERI

Mercenaries and professional soldiers have been employed in armies since ancient times. Alexander the Great used them in his extensive conquests. In the Middle Ages, "free companies" were often hired to fight feudal wars. Leaders of mercenary armies during the wars in Italy from the early 14th to the 16th century, called the condottieri, took their name from condotta, or contract, by which they agreed to serve a lord or city. Mercenaries were used because of the inefficiency of the communal militia and the desire of the merchant class to avoid personal military service. At first, the condottieri were often Catalan soldiers, but by the middle of the 14th century, most were Germans and Hungarians. Italian soldiers, members of the Malatesta and Sforza families, also fought for pay and often became the rulers of Italian cities. Venice hired its generals on long-term contracts and thus created loyal standing armies led by famous condottieri, such as Erasmo da Narni, called Gattamelata (1370-1443), and Bartolomeo Colleoni (1400-

EUROPE DIGEST FOR THE HURRIED TOURIST

1475). They often proved unreliable, however, selling their services to the highest bidder or turning to plunder at war's end. Criticized by many for their treachery and cowardice, the condottieri were replaced by more reliable national armies at the close of the Italian Wars. In the 17th century, mercenaries were gradually replaced in European armies by standing volunteer forces. Swiss, German, and Dutch troops, however, were often employed by the rulers of other countries. German mercenaries from Hessen fought for the British in the American Revolution. Swiss mercenaries recruited under the terms of special treaties (called "capitulations") between the Swiss cantons and foreign powers, fought in several European armies between the 15th and 19th centuries but were most important in France, where they served as personal guards to the kings. Such arrangements were prohibited by the Swiss government in 1874, an exception being made for the Swiss Guard of the Vatican, which was established in 1505 and continues to exist today. In recent times, mercenaries have been employed in African civil wars. "Soldiers of Fortune," a magazine published in the United States, addresses contemporary mercenaries.

ITALY

UMBRIA

Umbria is the homeland of St. Francis of Assisi.

Situated between Tuscany and Lazio, at the foot of Apennine Mountains to the east, it is called "the green heart of Italy." It is a peaceful region, the smallest in Italy, and the only one without a shore. It has many rivers, hills, and a mild climate. This is why it was one of the earliest populated areas in Italy. The Etruscan civilization settled there upon their arrival from Minor Asia and later gave birth to the Roman civilization. Other inhabitants were Celts, Piceni, and Sabines. After the colonization by the Romans, Umbrians were integrated into the Roman Empire, and received Roman citizenship. With the birth of Christianity, Umbria saw a great development of religious centers under the influence of Saint Benedict and the construction of many churches, basilicas, and monasteries. It is the cradle of the Franciscan movement, created by Saint Francis of Assisi. The Capital is Perugia, renowned for its university and its thousands of foreign students. Terni, Gubbio, Orvieto, Spoleto are medieval towns built on Etruscan settlements. Assisi is full of the memory of Saint Francis who lived there from 1182 to 1226.

BASILICA DI SAN FRANCESCO IN ASSISI

Started just after Saint Francis' death, and built by artisans from Rome and Florence at the end of 14th century, the Basilica contains magnificent 14th century frescoes painted by Cimabue and 28 frescoes on the life of St. Francis painted

EUROPE DIGEST FOR THE HURRIED TOURIST

by Giotto. Other major painters have worked in the Basilica, including Lorenzetti and Simone Martini. Great artists such as Luca Signorelli, Filippo Lippi, Perugino and Pinturicchio also worked in other churches and monasteries in Umbria. The Basilica dedicated to Saint Francis receives an average of 5 million visitors every year. This figure nearly doubled after the disaster of 1997. During the night of September 26, 1997, at 2:30 in the morning, an earthquake measuring 5.5 on the Richter scale shook a region of about 60 km in diameter around Assisi, devastating all of the villages and touching the Basilica. The lower Basilica suffered no damage, but in the upper Basilica, some 800 bits of frescoes fell down in the transept.

During the inspection conducted the following morning by two monks and civil engineers, a second quake of 5.8 shook the Basilica again, this time trapping and killing the monks and the workers. In Assisi, a total of 12 people were killed in the two quakes, and 38,000 people became homeless.

In 1226, one of the first disciples of Saint Francis, who was visiting the building site of the Basilica, exclaimed, "It is too luxurious. Francis would never have accepted it. One day or another, he will have it destructed." Some of the people in Assisi still think that the earthquake was the will of Saint Francis. For the Franciscan community, this prediction was absurd. Fortunately enough, the building did not collapse and suffered little outside damage. None of the stain glass windows fell down, the lower basilica did not suffer from the quake, and the 28 frescoes painted by Giotto on

ITALY

the sidewalls were not affected. The biggest damage was the collapse of the arch at the entrance, where are represented the four doctors of the Church, of some pieces of the central vault where Giotto painted the Saints, and a part of the second vault above the altar, painted by Cimabue. Restoration is now complete. A total of 180 square meters of frescoes had to be restored, involving the repositioning of 400,000 bits and pieces in order to restore the original pictures, all from photos and computer images. The eight saints of the entrance were completely restored in 2001. Also, all arches were reinforced to support future earthquakes. To this day, the Basilica has suffered 23 earthquakes; and the latest renovations and reconstruction efforts were designed to make it earthquake-proof.

LAKE TRASIMENE

This is the fourth largest lake in Italy with a surface of 50 sq miles and a depth of only 20 feet. It is famous for one of the most disastrous defeats in the Roman military history. During the second Punic war, in 217 BC, the Carthaginians, led by Hannibal, wiped out the Roman Army on the shores of the lake.

EUROPE DIGEST FOR THE HURRIED TOURIST

AREZZO: THE LEGEND OF THE TRUE CROSS

Arezzo is a Roman town and was one of the major Etruscan cities. During the middle ages and the Renaissance, many castles and churches were built there, but it suffered heavily from fighting during WWII. The cathedral escaped, with its beautiful series of frescoes illustrating the Legend of the True Cross, painted by Piero Della Francesca. Born around 1412, Della Francesca painted the Legend of the True Cross between 1452 and 1466. This work is recognized as being one of his major works.

Unfortunately, the fresco was executed on the walls of a church built in 1290 on the slope of a hill, which was unsteady and soaked with running water. Earthquakes, permanent infiltration of water in the walls, and the occupation of the church by Napoleon troops led to the deterioration of the masterpiece.

A first restoration was carried out in 1858, and a second one in 1910. A large quantity of cement was used to fill in the cracks and consolidate the panel, but the cement provoked a chemical reaction causing sulphur to accumulate, covering the painting with a white crust. The painting also blistered and cracked. In 1960, a new restoration attempt was launched, which did not bring any result. A second attempt in 1985 lasted four years. Finally, a professor from Florence found a way to stop and reverse the process: the walls were drained and dried; at the same time, a controlled micro-climate was created in the church. After a patient work of more than ten years, 20 sq m of the original 80 sq m have been restored to their original colors and luminosity.

ITALY

BOLOGNA

The main town of the Province of Emilia, Bologna has acquired many nicknames over the centuries:

The Learned: it is the home of Europe's oldest university, founded in 1088. Petrarch, Copernicus, Donizetti, Pico Della Mirandola, and Thomas Beckett studied there. Galileo applied for the chair of mathematics but was rejected (he got it in Pisa).

The Fat: it is considered the home of the finest and richest cuisine in Italy. This is the place where tortellini and tagliatelle were born. Tagliatelle is said to have been produced for the marriage of Lucrezia Borgia and the Duke of Ferrara. The long straw-colored pasta was inspired by the bride's flowing locks of hair.

The Red: because of the terracotta (baked red clay) used in buildings, or, as some people say, because the city was controlled by the Communists during most of the pre-WWII period.

The Turreted: because of its many towers. During medieval times, Bologna had as many as 200 towers; only 12 remain. If one is to believe the legend, two of the wealthy families competed to build the tallest and most beautiful towers. The Asinelli family probably won: their tower, built at the beginning of the 12th century, now stands 320 feet high and has 500 steps leading to the top. It was even taller than Pisa's tower, but the top part was removed once it began to lean. Bologna has not one but two leaning towers.

Bologna is famous for its porticoes: there are some 25 miles of them. Some people suggest they have been built to keep people dry, as Bologna has the record of being the wettest place in the country. The height of the porticoes was regulated to a minimum of 8½ feet, to allow men on horseback to pass underneath.

In the 4th century BC, the Boii, a Celtic tribe coming from Transalpine Gaul conquered the existing Etruscan settlement and the surrounding area . The tribe settled down and, after a period of aggressivity, mixed successfully with the Etruscans.

The city was conquered by the Romans during their phase of expansion, but accepted reluctantly the influence of the Roman Republic. With the outbreak of the Punic Wars, the Celts joined Hannibal's when he crossed the Alps, and gave him significant support. With the downfall of the Carthaginians came the end of the Boii as a free people. The Romans destroyed many villages, and founded the colonia of Bononia in c.189 BC.

During the Roman era, Bononia's population varied between c. 12,000 to c. 30,000.

After a long decline, Bologna was reborn in the 5th century under bishop Petronius who Christianized the area.

In 728, the city was captured by the Lombards, becoming part of the Lombard Kingdom.

In the 11th century, Bologna had the status of a free commune, belonging to the Lombard League. Like most Italian cities of that age, Bologna was torn by internal

ITALY

struggles related to the Guelph and Ghibelline factions, which led to the expulsion of the Ghibelline family of the Lambertazzi in 1274.

In 1294, Bologna was perhaps the fifth or sixth largest city in Europe, with 60,000 to 70,000 inhabitants.

The following years saw an alternation of Republican governments and Papal or Visconti restorations, while the city's families engaged in continual internal fighting.

In 1506, the Papal troops of Julius II besieged Bologna and sacked the artistic treasures of his palace. From that point on, until the 18th century, Bologna was part of the Papal States.

In 1530, in front of Saint Petronio Church, Charles V of Habsburg was crowned Holy Roman Emperor by Pope Clement VII.

The period of Papal rule saw the construction of many churches and other religious establishments, giving work to a multitude of artisans, painters, sculptors, and architects.

Napoleon made Bologna the capital of the Cispadane Republic. After his fall, Bologna was once again under the sovereignty of the Papal States, rebelling in 1831 and 1849 against the Austrian garrisons, which controlled the city until 1860. After a visit by Pope Pius IX in 1857, the city voted for annexation to the Kingdom of Sardinia on June 12, 1859, becoming part of the united Italy.

Famous people born in Bologna:

Guido Reni (1575 – 1642), painter and co-founder of the "school of Bolognese painters".

Marconi, inventor of the radio telegraph communication system.

Pier Paolo Pasolini, write and film director,

Gino Cervi, movie actor, famous for his composition in Don Camillo.

SAINT DOMINIC

Saint Dominic (1171 – 1221) lived and preached at approximately the same time as Saint Francis of Assisi. They were friends, and the two orders they created worked very often together. Born in Spain, where he studied and was appointed canon, later prior, Dominic came to Languedoc in 1203 to preach against the Albigensians, accused of heresy. In the summer of 1216, Dominic and his 16 of his companions laid down the rules of St Benedict as the foundation of their new Order. This meeting is known as "capitulum fundationis" – chapter of foundation. In December 22, 1216, Dominic received the formal approval of his order from Pope Honorius III. The Dominican order was now an established body within the church when Dominic returned to Toulouse. He spent the rest of his life either in Rome or in traveling. In 1218, he made a great tour (3,380 miles, entirely on foot) from Rome to Toulouse, Spain, and back, via Paris and Milan. In 1220, he toured Lombardy. On Pentecost in 1220 and 1221, the first and second general chapters of the order were held in Bologna. After a visit to Venice in 1221, Dominic died at Bologna and was buried in the San Domenico Church.

ITALY

PADUA

In the Middle Ages, Padua was known as a place of pilgrimage. It had the second largest university, after Bologna, founded in 1222; Galileo was among the professors. It was a busy city as well as a rich one. In 1304, Giotto was hired to paint the frescoes in the Scrovegni Chapel. Frescoes by Andrea Mantegna adorn the 13th-century Eremitani Church. Another Florentine came to Padua in 1444: Donatello worked here for nine years, creating bronze panels for the high altar located in the six-domed Basilica of St. Anthony, and the superb equestrian statue of the condottiere Gattamelata, who died in Padua in 1443.

According to legend, Padua was founded by the Trojan hero, Antenor. The town prospered under the Romans, who called it Patavium. Destroyed by the Lombards in 601, Padua recovered rapidly to become a prosperous and politically important free commune from the 12th to the 14th centuries. Padua's growth continued under rule by the Carrara family from 1318 to 1405. Francesco II di Carrara proclaimed himself Lord of Verona, and clashed with Venice: he was captured by the Venetians, imprisoned with his children, and all were murdered. Venice occupied the town in 1405, and Padua became part of the Venetian Republic until 1797, when it was taken by Bonaparte's troops and proclaimed a free Republic under the French. In 1813, Paduan territory was invaded by Austrian troops and was annexed to the Habsburg Empire until 1866, when the Italian Army entered the city. In October 1866, the province of Veneto was at last annexed to the unified Kingdom of Italy as a result of a plebiscite. During the 1915 to 1918 war between Italy and Austria, Padua was the general headquarters of the Italian King and the Supreme Command. In 1918, the Armistice was signed in a villa on the outskirts of the city, ending the Habsburg Empire.

SAINT ANTHONY OF PADUA

Saint Anthony the Hermit was born in Lisbon on August 15, 1195. He was a Franciscan monk and a church doctor. He was a very eloquent preacher and had a reputation as a miracle worker. He is best known today as the patron saint invoked to find lost articles. After serving as a missionary in Morocco, he returned to Europe, where he became distinguished as a biblical scholar and preacher. In art, he is sometimes shown holding a book and a lily branch, symbolizing his great erudition. He was buried in Padua in 1231, and canonized in 1232. The basilica which bears his name was built immediately afterwards. The Saint's tomb is behind the Titian altar in the Saint's Chapel, on the left side of the basilica.

The Condottiere Gattamelatta is also buried in the basilica, together with his son, in a chapel commissioned by his widow, now named the Chapel of the Most Holy, on the right side of the church.

ITALY

Prato Della Valle

This enormous square in the center of Padua was once the site of the Roman Theater. The area was known to become a swamp as soon as it rained, and it was decided at the end of the 18th century to turn it into a square, now one of the largest in Europe. The excavation brought to light the remains of the Roman Theater, which could be seen until the middle of the 19th century. The project was first to build an island on which a marketplace and shops would be erected, but they were later demolished to plant trees. A moat goes all round it, with 78 statues representing important Paduan people selected amongst the families who contributed to the construction costs. The foundations of the Roman Theater are still present, under the water filing the moat.

VENICE

It is possible that Venice (Venezia) might disappear in the near future. It is entirely built on sand and mud banks, sinking slowly and hopelessly into the sea. The level of water has increased by 75 cm since the 18th century. Since the inlet channels have been widened to let huge container carriers and tankers enter the lagoon in order to reach the Marghera industrial harbor, the tides have slowly destroyed the sand and mud-banks that have always protected the

EUROPE DIGEST FOR THE HURRIED TOURIST

city. Winter high tides from the Adriatic periodically submerge Venice, and Piazza San Marco can be flooded with 1 m of water some seven or eight times a year.

In 1970, after years of discussion, a pharaonic project named Mose (Moses) was launched with the help of UNESCO and a large number of states. It consists of building a movable barrier of 78 inflatable gates across the three inlets, which would raise at the period of high tide, and protect the lagoon from the rising sea (a similar flood defense scheme called the Thames Barrier protects London).

For the moment, Venice is here, in full glory and gild. Venice is a unique experience that you will remember for the rest of your life. Nowhere in the world is there anything so enchanting, so appealing, so sensual, so puzzling, and so grandiose as the Serenissima ("Most Serene") – as the City called herself in the past. Sometimes, the city stinks, many of the buildings are just ugly, winters can be really miserable, the pedestrian streets flood several weeks every year, and the tourists are skinned by the sly merchants and hoteliers – but you will be bewitched by Venice, as millions of people have been. Armies of visitors have written about its spell, including Goethe, Wagner, Mann, James, Rousseau, Byron, Browning, Dickens, Garibaldi, Hemingway, and many others. Even Hitler found the city beautiful. Historic Venice is comprised of 118 small islands. The city has a population of 330,000, but one-third of these people live on the mainland in Mestre or Porto Marghera. Venice is famous for its waterways – as some ambassador wrote it: "streets full of water". True, everything and everyone arrives

ITALY

in Venice on wheels but once at the Piazzale Roma, or at the railway station, all this mass of people, goods and even cattle, must proceed about the city by motorboats, water buses, curved-prow gondolas, or by foot. Chateaubriand, the French writer and poet, made the following unflattering comment: "a city against nature – one cannot take a step without being obliged to get into a boat." The Grand Canal is historic Venice's main traffic artery. It snakes through the city of Venice in a large S shape, linking the Saint Mark Basin on one end to the lagoon near the railway station on the other. This ancient waterway measures 3,800 meters (2.36 miles) long and ranges from 30 to 90 meters (about 100-300 feet) wide. In most places, the canal is approximately 5 meters (16 feet) deep. It is lined with magnificent gothic, Romanesque and byzantine buildings.

To travel from one end to the other on a *vaporetto* is a must. The vaporetto is the bus of Venice and the only means of transportation for the working people. There are more than 100 boats operated by a nationalized company. It is the best way to mingle with the population of Venice.

On these waterways circulates heavy traffic of an incredible variety of boats. Flat and heavy barges convey food and drink from their arrival point to the city center. Others take the garbage out of Venice. Taxis and private launches roar around, all compelled to a 5 mile per hour speed limit.

Gracefully maneuvering in this traffic, the gondolas are the eternal icon of Venice. It is difficult to imagine Venice without the gondola. This flat rowing boat is said to have a

EUROPE DIGEST FOR THE HURRIED TOURIST

Turkish origin. The gondola, traditionally painted in black, is 36 feet long and 5 feet wide. In the 17th and 18th centuries, there were 10,000 gondolas in Venice. Today, there are about 400. A ride in one is a prime experience of a Venetian visit, although tariffs can be dissuading.

The city is criss-crossed by some 117 smaller *rii* (canals), spanned by more than 400 small footbridges. The canals, some of which date back to the ninth century, have been deepened to allow the passage of larger boats, and they also act as the drains and sewers for Venice. Every year, a mountain of excrement falls into the canals. When the tide is low, one can see the orifices by which most of the city's sewage leaves the houses at the bottom of the edifices. More modern buildings have septic tanks, but there are also, visible in many places, the little closets used as lavatories jutting from the façades of old palaces, emptying themselves directly into the water beneath. Tons of muck goes into the canals every day. Add to that the dust, vegetable peels, animal matter, ash, paper, rubble and wreckage that are thrown into the canals, illegally of course, and you can imagine how thickly the canal beds are lined with refuse. This brings a particular smell to Venice, especially in the back quarters. It is half-drainage, half-rotting stone, a stink that gives the real Venetian amateur a reluctant pleasure. Canals are periodically cleaned: a section is closed, drained, and cleaning work takes place, as well as restoration of the buildings masonry under water line. This takes an enormous time, and the cleaning of the city progresses slowly. Still, although the civic authorities are necessarily obsessed with sanitation, this does not seem to bother the Venetians. During the hot days of summer, men dive from the quaysides or the bridges into the muck. Fortunately, much of the foul refuse of Venice, like the mud, is washed away by the tide; otherwise, Venice would be uninhabitable.

Venice is not a large city. It is about two miles long by one mile deep, and you can walk from one end to the other in one and a half hours.

Although tourism remains Venice's most important business, the modern city encompasses a newer, industrialized sector on the mainland, including Mestre and Marghera, the latter being Venice's commercial port. Shipyards, oil refineries, and chemical and metallurgical complexes contribute to the city's economy. Burano lace and Venetian glass are world-renowned. Lido Beach, on one of the seaward islands of the lagoon, is a famous bathing resort on the Adriatic Sea.

HISTORY OF VENICE

As the Western Roman Empire was collapsing, the Venetian land was constantly invaded by successive waves of Goths, Huns, Avars, Lombards, and other scavengers. Mainlanders fleeing barbaric brutality used to abandon their land and homes, and flee to the shelter of the lagoon. Eventually, they founded several permanent settlements on the islands. They brought with them their families, tools, furniture, and even the stones of their churches.

Refugees had to settle in an inhospitable surrounding

EUROPE DIGEST FOR THE HURRIED TOURIST

infested with mosquitoes, living on fish and water.

Gradually, they took possession of the islands; rights of property were granted, and the first council chambers were established, along with the building of churches. Their beginnings are hazy and unclear. It took many years for the lagoon to spring into life, and several centuries for those new men to stop quarrelling with each other, develop into a nation, and built the great city of Venice.

Somebody spoke once of "this new man, the American", and the German poet Goethe used exactly the same phrase to describe the first of the Venetians. They were pioneers, like settlers in the early American West.

The foundation of Venice is said to have occurred at noon on March 25, 421, with the bell stroke of the first dedicated church on the islet of Rialto (rivo alto "high shore"). At first a kind of patriarchal democracy, Venice turned into an aristocratic oligarchy of the tightest kind, in which power was strictly reserved to a group of patrician families. Executive authority passed first to this aristocracy, then to an inner Council of Ten, and later, more and more restricted, to a Council of Three, which was elected in rotation for one month. To prevent popular risings and personal dictatorship, the structure of the State was made tyrannical, ruthless, impersonal, and carefully mysterious. Venice was a sort of a police state, except that instead of worshipping power, it was terrified by it, and refused it to any one of her citizen. Even the Doge himself, the chief magistrate elected by the Great Council in a tortuous four-stage process, was carefully kept away from any

ITALY

real power, becoming nothing more than a gilded puppet.

With a population of no more than 140,000 people at its largest, Venice had to be a state of specialized talent. It has produced fine administrators, seamen, merchants, bankers, artists, architects, musicians, printers, and diplomats. There were no poets, hardly a novelist, or a philosopher. Her best generals were condottieri. Every minute of Venice activity was directed towards commerce, control of the sea, political stability, and acquisition of wealth and power. For many centuries, it was never short of men to fulfill these aims. The Republic was also sustained by a powerful company of artisans, denied of all political privilege or responsibility, but always governed fairly, and often generously.

Exploiting its natural maritime potential, Venice soon gained control of the Adriatic Sea, established outposts in the Levant and became a staging area for the Crusades. The Venetian doge instrumented in diverting the Fourth Crusade to conquer Constantinople in 1204. In 1275, the Venetian Marco Polo reached Peking, opening a trade route between Europe and the Far East. Thereafter, Venice became unique among nations, poised between Rome and Byzantium, between Christianity and Islam, one foot in Europe the other one in Asia. It was the unchallenged broker of most east-west commerce and cultural exchanges. Called Serenissima and decked in cloth of gold and Oriental fineries, it was the most flamboyant city in the world. Venice continued to grow in power. In 1380, it defeated Genoa, its only European rival for mastery of the seas. Venice arsenal was the supreme shipyard of the world: its walls were two miles round, and 16,000 people worked there. In the 16th century war against the Turks, a new galley left its yards every morning for 100 days. At the Battle of Lepanto n 1571, Venetian ships played an important role in the destruction of the Turkish fleet.

With the fall of Constantinople to the Turks in 1453, Venice lost a rich crenel of its eastern supremacy.

Overshadowed as a mercantile centre, first by the Portuguese discovery of an all-water route to the Far East around Africa and then by the growing importance of the Western Hemisphere, Venice went slowly into decline. Its Mediterranean Empire was lost, bit after bit, all to the Turks. By 1796, the population had fallen to 90,000; trade had vanished; and military power was reduced to use of their powder (when dry enough) for fireworks. Taken by the French troops commanded by General Buonaparte, the Republic of Venice dissolved, and was later attributed to Austria in 1797 by the Treaty of Campo Formio.

Venice fought unsuccessfully against this foreign domination throughout the Risorgimento, and was handed over to the Italian Kingdom by Bismarck in 1866, thanks to Italian support in the Prusso-Austrian war. This was the end of the Venetian entity.

Industrialization in the 20th century has brought about a new economic prosperity and rapid population growth in greater Venice. At the same time, however, the city's delicate ecosystem is threatened. Air and water pollution continue to erode the facades of many ancient monu-

ITALY

ments. Dredging of the lagoon to facilitate entry of large tankers has altered the natural cleansing action of the water movement. Each winter, severe flooding damages the foundations of many buildings. Efforts to save the historic city from physical collapse come from private funds and from international organizations, especially UNESCO.

THE VENETIANS

You can tell a Venetian by his face. Thousands of Italians live in Venice, but a trueborn Venetian is instantly recognizable. He might have some Slav blood, perhaps Austrian, possibly Asian heritage; he is different from the Latin. He often has a prominent nose, and he is sometimes bowlegged. He is a man of some reserve and carries a glance of complacency and sometimes of sly contempt. The Venetians seem to have the melancholic pride of people excluded from the fold of ordinary nations. They even have a language of their own, an original dialect mixture of various origins, including French, Arabic, Greek, German, and Latin, which only now are beginning to fade out under the impact of cinema and television. They are usually not boisterous and are polite without the usual Italian flattery. They consider the Venetian way as the right way, and they always know best. They are not boastful, only convinced.

There was a time when kings bowed before the Doge of Venice. An anecdote tells that Titian, the lordliest of the Venetian painters, once graciously allowed the Emperor

EUROPE DIGEST FOR THE HURRIED TOURIST

Charles V of Spain to pick up the paint brush he had accidentally dropped.

Today, modern Venice is not as preeminent as it would like: its glitters and sparkle all come with the summer visitors, and its private intellectual life is sluggish. There is not one genuine full-time theater, and concerts, except during the tourist season, are usually second-rate. Workmanship is variable, except for the glass-blowing factories, and the university is a mere department of the University in Padua. Nevertheless, Venetians love and admire their city. Visitors will, too, if they can grab the splendor and the melancholy of this jewel once on top of the world.

ART AND CULTURE

Venice's commitment to the arts is expressed in the Venice Biennale and in annual cinema, drama, and music festivals. Grand opera is still presented at the Teatro la Fenice, where works by Verdi, Rossini, Wagner, and Stravinsky were first performed.

Like its great rival Florence, Venice has acquired, as far back as the beginning of the Trecento, a new and original experience of gothic architecture, represented by the Doges Palace, Saint Mark's Basilica and the typical look of Venetian buildings. The immense wealth brought by trade with the Middle and Far East allowed the municipality to commission the best architects and decorators in Europe.

ITALY

Painting

Venetian painting rivals with Florence in the number of masterpieces, the originality of new designs and techniques, and fame.

From the 180 odd painters known to have worked in Venice until its fall in 1797, let us mention a few of the greatest artists of all times:

- Paolo Veneziano (c.1333 – c.1358), often called "the most important Venetian painter of the 14th century";
- Giovanni Bellini (c.1333 – 1516), considered as the founder of the Venetian school, and one of the first painters to introduce oil painting on canvas;
- Andrea Mantegna (c. 1431 –1506), experimented new approaches in the field of perspective;
- Vittore Carpaccio (1460 – 1526), imported Flemish techniques and styles;
- Jacopo Tintoretto (1518 – 1594), by real name Jacopo Comin, his dramatic use of perspective space and special lighting effects make him a precursor of Baroque art.
- Paolo Veronese (1528 – 1588), famous for paintings such as The Wedding at Cana, he is particularly know for the beauty of his green colors ("Veronese green"). Veronese was one of the first painters whose drawings were sought by collectors during his lifetime;
- Tiziano Vecelli (c.1488 – 1576), better known as

Titian, the most important member of the 16th-century Venetian school, he was equally adept with portraits, landscape backgrounds, and mythological and religious subjects.
- Giovanni Antonio Canal (1697 – 1768), better known as Canaletto, famous for his landscapes of Venice. He was also an important printmaker in etching.
- Giovanni Battista Tiepolo (1696 –1770), he was prolific, and worked not only in Italy, but also in Germany and Spain.

Theater and Music

It is true that Opera was born in Florence in 1600, and that Monteverdi composed "Orfeo" in Mantova seven years later, but lyric representations were then only given in private courts or palaces.

Venice was the first town where public theaters were built. The noble and rich families of Venice, rivaling with each other, started subsidizing theatres for the population of Venice, and in a matter of two or three years, more than 15 theatres were performing. Success was immediate. Over a period of 40 years, 436 original operas were composed.

Monteverdi brought the lyric art to the pinnacle. The end of the century saw the up rise of another genius: Antonio Vivaldi. A third creator for the Venetian stage, Carlo Goldoni, one of the fathers of comedy, was also born in Venice in 1707.

The most famous Italian opera house after La Scala in

ITALY

Milano, is Venice's La Fenice (The Phoenix). On January 29, 1996, an electrician working on restorations in the theater, unhappy to have to pay a heavy fee because of delays, decided to set a small fire – which he wanted to create only minor damages – in a room in the building. Unfortunately, the fire alarm had been disconnected because of the restoration work, and the canals around the theater had been emptied for cleaning. Before the Fire Department could intervene, it was too late, and La Fenice burned to the ground.

With the help of a large number of Italian and foreign contributors, it took seven years, to reconstruct La Fenice exactly as it was, except for the fireproof wooden materials, security measures, and modern scenic machinery.

WHAT TO DO IN VENICE

Organized tours include usually the visit of San Marco Basilica, the Palazzo Ducale (Doge's Palace), and a glass factory.

Individual travelers wishing a guided visit of these monuments can apply to the Venice Tourist office at: turismovenezia.it/eng, or call (+39) 0415298711. You can visit their pavilion to get a free map of the city, various leaflets, and other useful information: when standing facing St Mark's basin, between the two columns topped by the St Mark's winged lion and the statue of St Theodore (Saint Patron of Venice), turn right along the building, cross the gardens (Giardini Reali). The tourist office pavilion is in front of you. The office organizes also walking of the city

EUROPE DIGEST FOR THE HURRIED TOURIST

(on foot, of course), and gondola rides.

When on your own, according to the time you can spare, the choice is the following:

- Sit on the terrace of one of the cafes on St. Mark's Square, and watch other tourists walk by or pose for photos with pigeons (mind that prices for drinks are rather unfriendly). There are three cafés on the square with large outdoor sitting in full view of the Basilica and the Campanile, each with an orchestra playing alternatively. Florian opened in 1720 and is said to have been the first to serve coffee in Venice. Quadri's opened in 1775. Both have delightfully decorated lounges, air-conditioned in the summer, and offer excellent food, though expensive.

- Take the elevator to the top of the Campanile (314 ft) for a fantastic view of Venice.

- Take through the labyrinth of narrow streets from St Marks Square to the Rialto Bridge (or back). Plates indicate the direction, local residents walk this distance in ½ hour, see how much time it will take you…

- Take a gondola ride. Gondolas are expensive: a 40-minute's hire costs €80, each additional 20 minutes €40. After 7.00 pm, the price goes up,

ITALY

respectively €100 and €50. A gondola accommodates a maximum of six passengers. If you are by yourself or in a small number, it might be advisable to book a ride through the Tourist office, which charges €28/person for a 35 minutes ride. If you don't care for a ride, but wish to experiment the gondola, try the *traghetto* (ferry). These gondolas cross the Grand Canal at seven points between St Mark's square and the railway station. Of course, the ride takes only a few minutes, but it costs only €0.50 – a bargain.

- Take a ride on the vaporetto. The most interesting routes are n°1, which runs from Piazzale Roma to the Lido, with stops all along Grand Canal, and n° 2, an express line that circles Venice via the Grand Canal and the wide canal separating the central area and the Giudecca Island. Price for a single ticket, valid 60 minutes, is €6.50. Riding a vaporetto is really submersing into the Venetian every day's life, especially when employees, executives and office clerks commute to work.

- Visit a Murano glass selling shop. On St Mark's Square, there are many, selling everything from the glass bead necklaces to large mirrors or the famous Murano glass candelabras. Most of them have a small workshop featuring a furnace and a glass-blowing artisan, but this is just for demonstration to tourists. The whole production of glass is today located on the island of Murano. When entering a shop, check for the trademark "Vetro Artistico Murano", as some souvenir shops sell cheap Chinese counterfeits for original Murano glass. Prices are more or less the same everywhere, but purchasing an important item will request comparison amongst the different offers, or a visit to the galleries on the island of Murano, easily reachable by Vaporetto n°5, leaving from Zaccaria pier (near St Mark's square). Don't forget bargaining.

WHERE TO EAT

Corteo Sconta
Calle del Pestrin, Castello
Tel. 041 522 70 24
Delightful trattoria in a hidden courtyard. Prices from € 45.

Hotel Gritti
Tel. 041 79 46 11
Pure Venetian 18th century style, and a terrace on Grand Canal. Prices from € 80.

Harry's Bar
Tel. 041 528 57 77
Frequented by Hemingway in the late 1940s, this restaurant/bar is a must for the service, food, and the jet-set atmosphere. Prices expensive.

ITALY

Hotel Monaco & Grand Canal
San Marco 1332
Tel. 041 520 0211
Within a stone's throw from San Marco, the local, as well as the international clientele, choose this elegant restaurant for the view and the fare. Be sure to reserve a table on the terrace overlooking the Grand Canal. This is an unforgettable experience.

Prices are rather high, but, between the meal services, one can simply order a drink, or a sandwich.

Restaurant and Taverna San Trovaso
Fondamenta Priuli 1016
Tel. 041-520-3703
Vaporetto stop - Accademia
Reservations recommended, especially in the summer.
The San Trovaso attracts a mixed clientele of local residents, university students, and foreign visitors. Prices are mostly low (for pizza) to moderate (for à la carte items).

Many restaurants, trattorias, osterias, and pizzerias line the narrow streets around San Marco Square and Rialto Bridge, but should be scrutinized before entering, as the quality is not always up to the price.

SWITZERLAND

SWITZERLAND

OFFICIALLY NAMED THE Swiss Confederation, Switzerland is located in Western Europe, where it is bordered by Germany to the north, France to the west, Italy to the south, and Austria and Liechtenstein to the east.

Switzerland, also called the Helvetic Confederation, is a federal republic composed of 26 cantons (districts), with a total area of 15,700 sq mi and a population of 6.9 million.

The Swiss Confederation was established on August 1, 1291; Swiss National Day celebrates this anniversary.

It is the country of the Swiss Chalet, the Yodel, the Alphorn, steep cogwheel trains, chocolate, the Swiss Army knife, and, of course, the Swiss watch. Switzerland is also the center of the Alps, which extend in crescent from France over Switzerland to Austria and North Italy. The Swiss Alps comprise some of the highest and most well known mountains: the Jungfrau (13,642 ft), the Matterhorn (14,692 ft), and the Eiger (13,025 ft).

The main towns of Switzerland are:

Zurich - Switzerland's biggest city (365,000), and a

major center of banking, it also has a thriving nightlife. More than 95 banks have their headquarters or a branch in Zurich.

Geneva - This center of arts and culture, the second-largest city in Switzerland is by far the international capital, home to around 200 governmental and non-governmental organizations. Geneva was the home of John Calvin during the Reformation, elevating the city to the rank of Protestant Rome, the effects of which drive Geneva today.

Berne - The Swiss capital features an amazingly well preserved old-town with arcades along almost every street. The Swiss national gold reserve, amounting to 1,145 tons, is believed to be stored in huge vaults beneath the Federal Great Square, at an undisclosed depth of several dozens of meters. Restaurants abound, as do bars and clubs.

Basel - Slightly smaller than Geneva, Switzerland's third city is the traveler's gateway to the German Rhineland and Alsace in France.

Lausanne - While Geneva is busy being the international capital, Lausanne fills the role in most of the rest of French-speaking Switzerland. Scenery, dining, dancing, boating, and the Swiss wine-country are the draws.

Lugano – This is one of Italian-speaking Switzerland's top destinations, with a gorgeous old town on the shore of a beautiful lake. The food is simply amazing. This is the home (or refuge) of Italian millionaires.

Locarno – Smaller than Lugano, it is situated on the Lago Maggiore linking Switzerland to Italy. As in Lugano, a large number of wealthy Italian people have a residence here.

SWITZERLAND

Lucerne - Central Switzerland's main city with direct water links to all of the early Swiss historic sites is pretty and receives many tourists, but the views and museums make putting up with the crowds well worthwhile.

Interlaken - The outdoor and action sports capital of Switzerland offers anything from skydiving, bungee jumping, and hiking to whitewater rafting.

Zermatt - There are many mountain resorts in Switzerland, but only one of them has the Matterhorn Mountain. One of the most famous mountains in the world due to its pyramid shape, the Matterhorn was climbed for the first time on July 14, 1865. Led by Englishman Edward Whymper, four of the seven men lost their lives in the ascent.

Davos - The highest city in Europe and the largest ski resort of Switzerland, Davos hosts the annual World Economic Forum, gathering business, political, and academic leaders from around the world.

St. Moritz - World's oldest and most famous "exclusive" winter resort: cosmopolitan, pricey, fashionable and, above all, the place to be seen

Grindelwald – The Eiger, Jungfrau, and Mönch summits overlook this classic mountain resort, the Mecca of Alpine climbing.

Gstaad - Named "The Place" in the 1960s by Time Magazine, Gstaad is widely known for its famous part-time residents and vacationers. Crowned heads, business tycoons, movie stars, and famous artists mingle here on the slopes of one of the largest skiing domain in Switzerland

EUROPE DIGEST FOR THE HURRIED TOURIST

and in the exclusive hotels, restaurants, and shops.

Crans Montana – At an elevation of almost 5,000 ft above sea level, facing the giants of Valais Alps, this resort offers a skiing complex 87 m long, and one of the world's highest golf courses.

Switzerland is a small country and a place of transit between its neighbors. The great majority of the Swiss speak at least three languages. The Northern and Eastern regions speak English, French, and a dialect of German called Schweitzer Deutsch. The West region speaks French, German, and English, while the South speaks Italian, German, English, and French. The people of the cantons of Uri (the oldest canton of Switzerland) and Graubünden add to this combination Romansch, a local ancient dialect.

Switzerland is a peaceful, prosperous, and stable modern market economy with low unemployment, a highly skilled labor force, and a per capita GDP larger than that of the big Western European economies. It is also one of the safest states in the world.

At the same time when European Catholic and Reformed Nations were involved in bloody wars and massacres, the Swiss were inventing Gruyere cheese and the cuckoo clock.

Switzerland has been a neutral country since 1515, when the Swiss confederates, allied to the German Empire and Burgundy, were defeated by King François I of France. Switzerland then signed a perpetual peace treaty with France and never participated again in a war as a State. Their soldiers, renowned for their bravery and fighting

SWITZERLAND

skills, found employment as mercenaries in many European countries, especially in France, where they bravely died in service to the King during the French Revolution, and the Vatican, where they are still in charge of guarding the Pope.

Today, the Swiss Armed Forces are composed mainly of conscripts aged 20 to 34 (in special cases up to 50). Swiss citizens are prohibited from serving in foreign armies, with the exception of the Swiss Guards of the Vatican.

The structure of the Swiss militia system stipulates that the soldiers keep their own personal equipment, including all personal weapons, at home. All male Swiss citizens are bound to the military service. Women can serve voluntarily. After an initial training at the age of 18, conscripts serve periods of 18 to 21 weeks in boot camps, until the age of 34 (sometimes 50 for officers).

THE GOVERNMENT

The Federal Council (Bundesrat) is the seven-member executive council that constitutes the federal government of Switzerland and serves as the Swiss collective head of state. Each Councilor heads one of the seven federal executive departments.

Each year the Federal Assembly elects one of the seven councilors as President of the Confederation. The Federal Assembly also elects a Vice-President. By convention, the positions of President and Vice-President rotate annually, each Councilor thus becoming Vice President and then President every seven years while in office.

According to the Swiss order of precedence, the President of the Confederation is the highest-ranking Swiss official. He or she presides over Council meetings and carries out certain representative functions that, in other countries, are the business of the head of state. The President is not the Swiss head of state (this function is carried out by the Council in its entirety). However, the President now acts and is recognized as head of state while conducting official visits abroad.

The government rules by laws submitted to referendum of the population; this is the only country in the world to apply such a democratic rule.

SWISS ACHIEVMENTS

Swiss citizens have contributed greatly to the world knowledge, art, and culture: John Calvin – Jean Jacques Rousseau – Pestalozzi, the educational reformer – the novelist Hermann Hesse – the sculptor Giacometti – the painter Paul Klee – the architect Le Corbusier, and Jean Henri Dunant, the humanitarian businessman who founded the Red Cross in 1864. He received the first Nobel Prize in 1901. Not to forget Zino Davidoff, a refugee from Ukraine in 1911, established in Geneva, who brought his line of Cuban cigars to world fame.

Switzerland was also temporary residence to Vladimir Illych Ulyanov (Lenin), who lived there until 1917.

Although a tiny country, Switzerland proves mighty in many domains:

SWITZERLAND

Banking

The banks, famous for the secrecy they provide to their customers. This secrecy, however, is today somewhat dented by the pressure put onto the Swiss Banking system by the United States and leakage instigated by French, or other foreign tax administrations.

It is believed that treasures from Hitler's Germany lie there in complete anonymity. Recently, it was discovered that belongings of the Jews exterminated by the Nazis were deposited in various accounts. Switzerland promised to return them back to their heirs and has started doing so. But how many families will be able to claim these belongings, when so many disappeared completely without a lineage? Nazi Germany has disappeared, and there is no one to claim these deposits, so the Swiss Banks can continue to profit from that money forever.

Pharmacy

Important laboratories in the chemical dye and pharmaceutical industry produce a large percentage of the world's medication products, and pharmaceutical research is one of the most advanced in civilized countries. Ciba-Geigy ranks the seventh world producer, and Sandoz the 9th.

Watch industry

Despite Japanese competition, Swiss watches represent 75% of the world industry. The Swiss keep their rank as the best watch manufacturers (and also some of the most expensive, apart from Swatch, which produces a cheap "use and throw" line).The demand for expensive watches doubled between 1990 and 2000, when Switzerland exported a record 10 billion Swiss francs for 30 million pieces. A watch is the gift by excellence: Poutine was offered a Breguet Flight Model watch by President Chirac.

High precision industry

Electronic devices, laboratory equipment are well renowned; the SIG SAUER pistols are accepted for being some of the best handguns in the world, and OERLIKON artillery guns have a long established reputation of reliability.

Atomic and physic research

Geneva hosts the world's largest laboratory, the CERN (Conseil Européen pour la Recherche Nucléaire), dedicated to particle physics research.

Chocolate

Today, Swiss chocolate manufacturers enjoy a world reputation. Chocolate was introduced as a drink from the New World in the 17th century. It was only in the mid-19th century that production of chocolate bars started; by 1876, Switzerland produced milk chocolate bars on a commercial scale. Today, Nestlé is the biggest manufacturer of chocolate products in the world.

SWITZERLAND

THE SWISS ARMY KNIFE

In the 19th century, Carl Elsener, son of a hat maker, decided to take the profession of knife making. After his apprenticeship in Germany and France, he returned home in 1884 at the age of 24 and started his own workshop in Ibach, near Schwyz.

There was not much industry in this region at the time; potential workers used to emigrate. To create steady employment, Carl proposed to his colleagues cutlers to found the Association of Swiss cutlers with the aim of manufacturing knives for the Swiss Army, which were then bought in Solingen, Germany. The first delivery to the Army was made in 1891. The knives were very solid but also quite heavy, so Elsener created a more elegant and lighter knife for the officers. This new knife, named called the "officer's knife", was registered on June 12, 1897. In 1909, after his mother's death, Elsener chose her name, Victoria, as a trademark. In 1921, the trademark Inox was added, creating the final name of Victorinox.

Today, more than 100 different models are manufactured in Ibach, where 950 workers are employed. The daily production of officers' knives totals 34,000 pieces per day (7 million per year). Including all of the other models of knives and cutlery (800 in all), the total production per year is 25 million pieces. From 1945 to 1949, Victorinox knives have been delivered in great quantity to the U.S. Army, Navy, and Air Force.

The name Offiziersmesser was too difficult to pronounce, so they were simply called Swiss Army Knives. Lyndon Johnson bought and offered 4,000 Victorinox knives to his guests at the White House. This tradition continued with Ronald Reagan and George Bush. When pilot Gary Powers was grounded by the Russians in 1960, among his personal effects displayed to the media was a Swiss Army Knife. The knife went to the moon as part of the equipment for NASA astronauts. In addition, last but not the least, think of all that Mc Gyver could do with his Swiss Army knife! The biggest Victorinox knife is the Swiss Champ 1.6795.XAVT. This knife costs CHF 364 ($400) and has 80 functions.

The red color and the white cross are registered and can be used only by Victorinox and Wenger, another Swiss manufacturer that went bankrupt and was bought by Victorinox in 2005.

SWISS HOSPITALITY

The Swiss have always had a keen sense of hospitality. Tourist and hotel industry has developed to a level of excellency, and graduates from Swiss hotel schools, such as the Cesar Ritz College, are always in great demand.

Cesar Ritz, "the king of hoteliers and hotelier for kings" (1850 - 1918), created the concept of luxury hostellery and opened the Ritz Hotels in Paris, London, and Madrid.

The Golden Tulip chain of hotels has its headquarters in Geneva, as well as the well-reputed Mövenpick chain of restaurants.

SWITZERLAND

FOOD

Foods often associated with Switzerland include cheese, such as Gruyère, Vacherin, and Appenzeller, and chocolate.

Fondue has a little gone out of fashion in Western Europe, but is still a part of Swiss cuisine. The classic fondue is bread dunked in Emmental and Gruyère cheeses mixed with white wine, potato flour, and a dash of nutmeg.

Rösti is a popular delicacy of shredded fried potatoes. It either comes as a garnish, or topped with fried eggs as a main dish.

Swiss bakeries offer a wide variety of bread rolls.

One specialty not to miss is the **Zürcher Geschnetzeltes**. However difficult it is to pronounce, this is a delicious preparation of thin strips of veal with mushrooms in a cream sauce, served with rösti.

LUCERNE

Capital of the Swiss canton of the same name, Lucerne (population 60,000) lies about 25 miles southwest of Zurich on the shore of the magnificent Lake of Lucerne, and the River Reuss. The lake, called also the Lake of the Four Cantons, borders the three original Swiss cantons of Uri, Schwyz, and Unterwalden. The waters of Lake Lucerne are reputedly so clear that you can drink them. All around the lake is a glorious vista of some of Switzerland's best-loved mountains, the Pilatus Mountain on one side, and the

EUROPE DIGEST FOR THE HURRIED TOURIST

Rigi Mountain on the other.

Serenaded by yodelers and alphorns, Lucerne is a tourist attraction that combines all the clichés about chocolate, cheese, and cuckoo clocks, showcased in an idyllic Alpine setting of lakes and mountains. The central Swiss city has been a must on every tourist itinerary of Switzerland since Queen Victoria visited it in 1868 and was bowled over by the stunning panoramas, crystal water, and clear air.

Lucerne claims to have the world's largest fleet of paddle steamers, which have operate since 1837. All of the cities along the lake are ports of call for the Lake Lucerne Navigation Company. The magnificent vintage vessels offer a beautiful approach to the surrounding scenery. The admiral ship Schiller, built in 1906, was restored and overhauled in 2000 at a cost of 6 million Swiss Francs. Its classical superstructure, elegant interior and precision engines make the trip an unforgettable moment. One of the most popular combinations is a Golden Round Trip excursion by boat to the village of Alpnachstad, followed by a climb up Pilatus mountain culminating in 2,132 m by the steepest cogwheel railway in the world and back by cable car, cabins and bus or train to Lucerne (visit pilatus.com for more information).

On the other side of the lake, Rigi mountain 1,800 m, can be climbed either by cable car or by cogwheel railway. The combined trip by paddle steamer from Lucerne, then by cable car, and back by cogwheel railway is also a very nice excursion (see rigi.ch).

Lucerne was settled around the monastery of Saint Leodegar in the 8th century, which belonged to the Abbey of Murbach in Alsace, France. It flourished as a trade center when it was sold by the Abbott to the Habsburg in 1291. In 1332, it joined the Swiss Confederation, and an alliance of town folks and peasants formed against the Habsburgs. The resistance went on for 54 years until a final victory was achieved by the Swiss confederates. It served as the capital of the Helvetic Republic between 1798 and 1803.

The old wall with nine towers is a remaining part of the fortifications around the town, built around 1400.

Lucerne is not a big town. Its center can be easily visited on foot, enjoying the peaceful atmosphere of the old streets lined with painted houses, cozy cafés, restaurants, and shops not surprisingly oriented towards selling watches, Swiss army knives, and cuckoo clocks. One should not leave Lucerne without paying a visit to Bücherer, a seven-story high department store where an incredible choice of Swiss and foreign articles can be found, from a postcard to the latest Rolex.

Kapellbrücke

Lucerne's most photographed attraction, pictured on virtually every postcard, are the Chapel Bridge, built in 1333, and its Water Tower, which used to serve as both watch tower and prison cum torture chamber. It is the oldest wooden bridge in Europe.

In August 1993, the Chapel Bridge was almost completely destroyed by a fire, apparently started by a cigarette thrown from a passing boat. After eight months of restoration, the city's landmark reopened in 1994. The flames devoured many of the 110 gable paintings on the bridge that gave graphic details of the martyrdom of Lucerne's two patron saints, St. Leodegar and St. Mauritius, and the city's history. Experts were able to salvage only 30 of the works, and city leaders decided against filling the gaps with replicas. Nevertheless, the reconstruction cost 5 million Swiss Francs ($5.3 million).

The Lion Monument

It is the oldest surviving statue monument in Switzerland. It commemorates the self-sacrifice of the Swiss Guard during the Tuileries Riot in Paris in 1792. The idea came from one of the guards who escaped the massacre on leave. The monument was carved in 1821.

Lucerne also houses one of the largest transport museums in Europe.

LUCERNE RESTAURANTS

Hotel Des Balances
Weinmarkt
Tel. 418-28-28
Prices: Main courses 27F-57F; fixed-price dinner 79F-95F

Reservations recommended.

The restaurant at this hotel in Altstadt, opening onto the historic Weinmarkt, is exceptional. The building was once the town jail but was converted into a restaurant in 1519. Its terrace, with a view of the river Reuss and the Chapel

SWITZERLAND

Bridge, is one of the most hotly contested seats in town on a balmy summer night.

Old Swiss House
Tel. 410-61-71

Prices: Main courses 18F-58F, lunch 34F-56F, fixed-price dinner 79F.

This half-timbered building near the Lion Monument is one of the most photographed attractions in the area. This crowd-pleaser has been a mandatory stopover on a dining tour of Lucerne since it started attracting a horde of British visitors in 1859. The restaurant is decorated in 17th-century style, with porcelain and antique glass, hand-carved oak doors, wooden stairways, leaded- and stained-glass windows with heraldic panes from 1575, antique silver, and old pewter. The house has a long bar near the entry, private banquet rooms upstairs, and a dining room downstairs. In fair weather, you can have lunch on the terrace. Wiener Schnitzel, Beef Stroganoff or Zürcher Geschnetzeltes can be found on the menu.

Rathaus Brauerei
Tel. 410-52-57

Prices: Main courses 16F-40F; beer 4F-8F

This is one of the few establishments in Lucerne that brews its beer on-site. It's located under the arcades of the riverfront promenade, close to the northern terminus of the well-known covered bridge, immediately beneath the exhibitions of the Picasso Museum. You can dine in the open air, or head inside to a series of medieval vaults that shelter the polished copper of the fermentation vats.

Schiffrestaurant Wilhelm Tell
Landungsbrücke 9
Tel. 410-23-30
Main courses 17F-28F
Reservations recommended

Built in 1908, this lake cruiser sailed boatloads of happy passengers from one end of Lake Lucerne to the other. After it was replaced by newer ships in the late 1960s, it was transformed into a floating restaurant in 1972. Now permanently moored at one of the quays, it's usually ringed with a colony of swans, which feed off the scraps thrown overboard. Drinks and snacks are served on outdoor cafe tables in the bow area, where you can have a beer or coffee throughout the day. A formal restaurant is found under the low ceiling of the aft section, where fine food is served with alert attention. The ship's engine, brightly polished and set behind glass, is on display as a work of industrial art.

Stadtkeller (City Hall)

Phone: 041/410-47-33 Prices: Main courses 45F-50F; fixed-price lunch 54F-65F; fixed-price dinner 67F-78F. Music surcharge for lunch or dinner imposed on a la carte meals and drinkers only.

Rated by many visitors as the Swiss equivalent to a beer hall in Munich, this cellar restaurant in the City Hall opened in 1685. Lined with antique accessories, it offers alpine meals whose flavors are enhanced by doses of folk music, which begins at 12:15pm for lunch and at 8pm for dinner. The most economical way to enjoy the place is simply to order half a liter of beer, with a supplemental charge imposed whenever music is playing. To really get into the experience, consider the heaping platters of smoked pork with sauerkraut, pork or veal sausages with rösti, several kinds of schnitzel with mushrooms, or roulade of beef with new potatoes. Folk music is featured only from March to October.

ON THE ROAD FROM LUCERNE TO GOTTHARD

The road over the St Gotthard Pass has been one of the major traffic axis between northern Europe and Italy since the early 13th century.

The N°2 Motorway links Lucerne with the St Gotthard Pass, following the southern side of the lake. It presents no visual interest.

The old historical road along the northwestern side of the lake passes along Rigi Mountain and offers an approach to historical sites such as the Field of Rütli on the opposite side, where the Swiss Confederation was founded in 1291. Representatives of the three valleys of Uri, Schwyz, and Unterwalden met there to seal the alliance. According to tradition, this meeting took place in the presence of William Tell.

A little further south, after Sisikon, Tell's Chapel commemorates William Tell's escape from the Bailiff Gessler's boat taking him to jail.

Flüelen is a port located at the southern end of the lake where customs duties were paid for all those using the Gotthard transit.

Altdorf is the Capital of the Uri Canton. In front of the City Hall is the famous monument to William Tell, erected in 1895, reminding visitors that this was his birthplace and home.

On the hill at Wassen is the church of St. Gallus. Travelers heading southbound stopped here to pray before going up the St Gotthard pass; those travelling northbound stopped to thank the Lord for a safe passage.

The St Gotthard pass (2,108m), the most famous of all the Alpine passes, is the border between the German speaking part of Switzerland and the Swiss Italian speaking canton of Ticino. Foot traffic had used the pass since about 1200, and the first carriage crossed in 1775. The pass road above is impassable in winter, and less than a century later in 1872, after decades of debate over routes and costs, work began on a rail tunnel beneath the pass. The first trains ran through the 15km-long tunnel in 1882. This line is still a vital north–south artery, carrying at peak times an average of one train every six minutes – with five million passengers and 25 million tons of freight carried each year.

The St Gotthard road tunnel, completed in 1980 after

SWITZERLAND

eleven years of construction, is – at 16.3km – the longest road tunnel in the world, and it remains open year-round.

Another example of Swiss engineering is the new railway tunnel under the St Gotthard, which will be the longest tunnel in the world, linking Zurich and Milano. After 17 years of work deep under the surface of the earth, drilling on the Gotthard Base Tunnel was completed on October 15, 2010. It will be years before the first trains roll through the 57 kilometer-long tunnel, but given the difficulties that workers have encountered, it is a wonder they have come this far. Workers of 10 different nationalities removed fully 24 million tons of rock (five times the volume of the Great Cheops Pyramid) in the drilling of the tunnel, which is actually a pair of tunnels, each 10 m in diameter, lying 40 m apart.

Indeed, were all the tunnels, including the cross tunnels, to be added together, they would extend for 153 kilometers. Up to 2,600 people worked concurrently on the project deep under the earth's surface, battling with the dust, noise, humidity, and temperatures of 30 degrees Celsius (almost 90 degrees Fahrenheit). It is estimated that 300 trains will circulate daily in the tunnel, at a speed of 250 km per hour for passenger trains and 160 for freight trains.

ADDITIONAL WEB RESOURCES

www.insightguides.com
www.timeout.com
www.europeforvisitors.com
www.virtualtourist.com
www.lonelyplanet.com

LONDON
www.ukguide.org
www.londonnet.co.uk

AUSTRIA
www.aboutaustria.org
www.wikitravel.org/en/Austria

FRANCE
www.discoverfrance.net

EUROPE DIGEST FOR THE HURRIED TOURIST

GERMANY
www.justgermany.org

ITALY
www.wikitravel.org/en/Italy

SWITZERLAND
www.wikitravel.org/en/Switzerland

BIBLIOGRAPHY

The Oxford History of Medieval Europe – Oxford University Press

Michelin Green Guides, 1 Parkway South Greenville SC 29615, USA.
www.travel.com
Available guide-books in English: Austria, Germany, Great Britain, France, Italy, Switzerland, London, Rome, Tuscany, Venice, French Riviera, Provence.

A year in Provence, by Peter Mayle (1989) — Pan Books London

French or Foe, by Polly Platt – Culture Crossings Ltd London

City Secrets: Rome, by Robert Kahn – Mill Hill Books

The Civilized Shopper's Guide to Rome, by Pamela

EUROPE DIGEST FOR THE HURRIED TOURIST

Keech and Margaret Brucia – The Little Bookroom, New York

Venice, by James Morris – Faber Editions London

CPSIA information can be obtained at www.ICGtesting.com
Printed in the USA
BVOW022341080212

282535BV00008B/4/P

9 781432 775339